Heaven in My Hands

A Midwife's Stories of Birth & Life

NANCY SPENCER

Book Vine Press
2516 Highland Dr.
Palatine, IL 60067

Dedication

To all the sweet babies who have graced my life.
To the great God in heaven who makes it all possible.

Acknowledgments

All the families who have come my way over the years have added immeasurably to my peace and happiness, and I especially wish to recognize them for their love and constancy. There are thousands of more stories behind the ones written here, and they are all precious.

My thanks to all the midwives I have known. Their courage and confidence is an inspiration always. Especially, I recognize two dear friends—Toni Erickson, whose generosity and love are legendary; and Laura Hamilton, whose common sense and virtue are deeply endearing. I learned "Safe and Happy" walking with these wonderful women.

Over the years, my physician friends have kept midwifery alive and safe: Dr. Kurt Weis, OB/GYN, who pioneered physician/midwifery collaboration in this area; Dr. Michael Smith, OB/GYN, greatly regarded for his accessibility and encouraging spirit; Dr. Arthur Maslow, Perinatologist/OB/GYN, who is every midwife's absolute favorite, (every patient's as well); and Dr. Jennie Hendrie, Pediatrician who loves midwives and is loved right back.

To my friend Molly Venzke, who first suggested we travel this literary road together, and through three of her babies later, I still lean on her editorial stills and her friendship.

Patti Ramos
Pamela Sweet
Karen Wolfe

These three women are accomplished photographers, and their contributions have added greatly to the stories in this book. I am grateful for their time and generosity, and their remarkable expertise with a camera.

To my brother, Kevin Twohy, a gentle warrior and a bright mind, whose optimism carries the day. Any good thing is possible.

To my family—especially my sons, Dr. Nathan Spencer and Dr. Daniel Spencer—who, in those early years as babies, got carried in the front pack and the backpack to many births.

To my husband, Donald His patience and his love for me are only bested by his love for God. Am I ever blessed!

Contents

Foreword

There are literally thousands of books about birth—how to do this or that, the birth process, fetal development, what-not-to-do's, and on and on. None, however, tell the story through the lens of the family and the events of their lives during the pregnancy, birth, and beyond as succinctly and beautifully as *Heaven In My Hands*. These are compelling stories of love, real life, and fidelity culled from decades of experience by Nancy Spencer, a marvelous practitioner of obstetrics and a woman who seems able to find God's presence "in all his distressing disguises," as Mother Theresa once said.

The Celts believed that one could most reliably experience God at the "thin places" of the world. Those places where land met water, light met darkness, birth met life, and life moved into death to become part of life again. At the physical, spiritual, and emotional levels, birth is very much a welcoming of the sacred, the ineffable, for anyone who's been fortunate enough to be present.

Welcome to a "thin place." Stay and enjoy Nancy Spencer's loving glimpses of that which cannot be named!

—A.S. Maslow

Arthur Maslow, DO, is a board-certified perinatologist who specializes in fetal ultrasound. While employing state-of-the-art ultrasound technologies to evaluate the developing heart of the fetus, he also strives to offer prospective patients as much information and guidance as possible. Dr. Maslow is a published author, member of The American College of Obstetricians and Gynecologists, served as the department director at several hospitals, and was an assistant clinical professor at the University of Washington. His specialties include maternal-fetal medicine, perinatology, and obstetrics and gynecology.

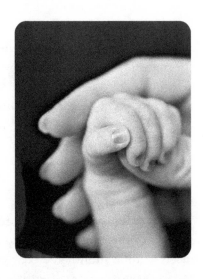

The Invitation

Life. Its sweet presence is everywhere. The sounds of life reverberate in a jumble of music—sometimes a shrill call of the whippoorwill, the meow of a Persian curled up in the sunshine, the happy shouts of children on the ball field, the yip of a Yorkshire terrier at play. The smells of life surely enrich every moment, from the purple heather climbing the hillocks to the fragrant peat at the bottom of the bog or the lavender catching the wind as streaming crowds gather at a summer festival along the Mississippi. The look of life lights the darkness: lovers holding hands as they walk through the park, old men playing checkers, young boys playing marbles, girls giggling about a shared secret. Every aspect of our existence is saturated with life as this magnificent globe spinning on its axis teems with this powerful force.

Sometimes the busyness of daily routines dampens the awareness of the life that resonates all around us, but it only takes the sight of the dandelion that has forced its way through a cement sidewalk to remind us of life's tenacity. A drive through the countryside during a flash spring shower, smelling the fresh, piney scent of evergreen gives us pause. A sparrow's song at sunrise suddenly awakens us to the dulcet sound of life's serenity. We are wrapped in a mantle of awe at all the beauty around us. But there is one particular experience, it seems, transcending all others; one moment of life more profound than any other. A baby's first breath, that primal cry of a brand-new human being, is so powerful, so rich, and so pure, it brings instant tears. The cycle of life begins anew—full of expectation, hope, and love.

The magic of this miraculous moment is tangibly spicy; its taste is in the air, and the aroma of this new life clings to everyone present. Proof of the life conceived nine months before pops his little head out, gasps his breath, and begins to vocalize his unique, God-given song. Then, within moments, he is peering into the eyes of his mother and father, soon to mimic expressions that resemble their own. As his parents put their heads and hearts together to marvel over this new little being, there exists a moment suspended in time of sheer purity, a shining light whose brilliance lingers in lovely shades of rosy pink. As this new child takes that first most important breath, the dusky hue of his brand-new skin disappears, replaced with a rich and glorious pink, like the freshest sunrise; truly the hope of the future rests in his small hands. The air is suffused with joy and delight and praise and beauty unparalleled.

Over nearly forty years of catching babies, touching the very presence of heaven in my hands, I have kissed about four thousand new little ones so far. The awesome impact of that first breath upon my heart never wanes. Every baby is magnificent, beautiful, perfection itself. His grand entrance into this world is never commonplace. How could it be? No matter what the physical surroundings of the actual birth or the life challenges these parents currently face, for those several minutes it seems as if everyone is momentarily enshrouded with a gauzy tent filled with the ambiance of heaven. For many parents, these moments linger, for a time stretching into days and weeks, like the remembrance of sweet perfume. For others, the daily necessities and challenges of living quickly begin to pierce this shroud, returning them to the reality of today. Whatever the duration, this momentary encounter with holiness is undeniable, a treasured memory forever.

This intimate journey we take together over nearly nine months deepens my love and affection, my respect and regard for these families. Many times there is the great blessing of more babies to come, and soon I feel like a member of the family. What an indescribable privilege, for my friends have graciously invited me to become woven into the fabric of their pregnancy and birth experiences, their very lives.

I am constantly amazed at the strength, the courage, the commitment each mom possesses. Simply to make the choice to take on the challenge of an unmedicated labor is bravery itself amidst a pop culture determined to avoid pain at any cost. But my moms have come to understand that birth is a perfectly designed event—a day, or more often a night, of hard work; like baling hay or rototilling an acre of a garden. When she is done, she knows she has done a grand piece of work. She knows there is something critically important about the work of labor itself, that the process has value as it informs the whole experience.

When labor begins, each woman steadies herself for the challenge, understanding the pain but ready to welcome the end result. This lovely woman is willing to sweat and strain through the intense physical workout of labor in order to provide the best possible introduction to the world for her baby. She knows him intimately, though she has not yet met him face-to-face. She could describe the feel of his toes under her ribs, the roll of his back as he moves side to side, the hardness of his little head against the press of her pelvis, the rhythmic thumping of his occasional hiccups. She calls him by name and longs to kiss his neck, to wrap her hands around his little fingers, to feel the softness of his cheek. The work is but a moment but so worth the effort for a lifetime.

Birth is often surprisingly clean, sometimes thoroughly messy, always perfectly designed, wonderfully unique, and completely unforgettable. Some births are filled with humor and laughter, some with sadness, some with surprise, some with a poignant tenderness. Some are noisy, some very still and quite. Some births are memorable for their particular, and occasionally peculiar, circumstances.

All in all, there is no such thing as a boring birth. When a baby is born, his head is pointed, his nose is too big, his ears are curled over, his eyes don't focus—and yet he is the most spectacularly beautiful creature ever born!

Every woman who births has a story to tell full of accomplishments, exploits, failures, celebrations, sorrows, and joy. In birth, each mother brings her distinctive personality and passion for life. Throughout the several months of care, I am privileged to come to know their unique stories and, for a period, become a participant in them. I fall in love with them, for these women and men have inspired me, informed me, and motivated me to pursue excellence. I have been deeply influenced by their tenacity, heroism, steadfastness, and unconditional love.

I have seen women risk their lives in order to give their unborn babies a chance for life, watched couples face uncertain odds in order to conceive a child, observed a young woman unselfishly bring forth a baby she knows she will not raise. I have been privileged to know parents who choose to walk through the intense grief of death so they may rejoice as their baby takes his one and only breath. There are fathers who change jobs to be more involved with their emerging families, or the young dad who takes responsibility for this new baby when it would be easier to walk away. I have welcomed families traveling long distances and making definitive sacrifices to achieve their desired birth plans. I have been blessed to witness thousands of couples introduce their Little Sweet Pea as a new member of the family while everyone rejoices.

The telling of these stories is important, I believe, to hand down the legacy of generosity, character, sensitivity, and humor. I dream about my wonderful families, and their experiences play over in my heart as I awaken to a sweet thought, a picture in my mind, a feeling of gratitude. It is such a transforming event. Though the names are often changed in these true accounts, these parents have extended an open invitation; you are welcomed to each of their births, to cherish the celebration of life, to be enriched by their stories, and to enjoy the moment when life changes everything.

The Baby Is Coming...Now!

Snow had been falling hard that Thanksgiving season for four days straight. The trees were heavy with snow, their limbs bending down nearly to the ground, the air shrouded in gray and absolutely still. Birds that sang lustily a month prior had long since flown south or were hiding in the corners of the barn or under the eaves, waiting for a breath of blue sky not soon to come.

A five was keeping us company in the brick hearth, the smell of cedar filling the room with sweetness, the pop and crackle of logs accompanying the chink of Scrabble tiles in our never-ending game. Suddenly a yellow Volkswagen roared up the long, winding driveway past out house and screeched to a halt just beyond the front door. The driver jumped out, leaving the car running with its heater blasting, and rushed up to the house, crying, "She's having a baby!"

Cheryl was not my patient. I had been her helper with her first baby, a three-day marathon in a doctor's clinic in Lynnwood. Cheryl planned to deliver there again, but clearly she wasn't going to make the drive. Soon after starting on the highway toward Lynnwood, her mother had recognized the signs of impending birth, and instead of heading north, she arrived unannounced in my driveway, with her daughter shouting from the car, "Come and help me!"

I dropped the Scrabble tiles and snatched up my midwife bag, always ready in the closet by the front door. As I quickly grabbed some gloves from the box and dashed out to help her, I could hear Cheryl hollering from the car. The urgency in her voice spurred me to readiness. Cheryl's baby was indeed coming.

As I lifted her ample skirt, her baby's black hair began to peek out. I calmed Cheryl with little "sh sh sh's," a moment of peace in the rush of delivery. With the next contraction, her sweet baby eased into towels in my arms, and I gently laid her down on the floorboards beneath her mother's feet. The noisy Volkswagen heater was a blessing that cold, wintry day, keeping tune with the baby's loud and full-throated cries. I cut the cord, wrapped SuzieMae in thick flannel towels, and handed her to her grateful grandmother, who quickly brought her into the house.

Getting Cheryl out of the bucket seat was a challenge. Trying to keep the discharge contained, with the cord and placenta wrapped into her skirt, we walked carefully to the house a short distance away. As we managed to fall across the threshold into the living room, Cheryl began to giggle. She was so amazed, so happy, so relieved, and so charged by this rush of events, all she could do was laugh out loud.

I think often of my friend Cheryl, who suddenly burst upon the calm of my life that wintry Thanksgiving in 1970. Her birth continually reminds me of the normalcy as well as the beauty of this experience, the humor that smiles around the edges, and the indescribable purity of that first cry. My midwife career was just beginning then, and I reflected later that this was a pretty awesome send-off.

Without a doubt, the emotional atmosphere of birth has always seemed positively charged, full of crackling electricity. There is a heightened sense of mystery, surprise, and anticipation. Cheryl couldn't possibly have planned that day as it happened. But looking back, it just seemed perfect.

Though today many events in our culture are planned with studied precision, birth continues to be suffused with an air of complete spontaneity. Who knows if it will be a boy or a girl? Or twins? You don't know until you know—and then it's still usually a surprise. Who knows when labor will begin? Or why? Or why not? Will day or night grace this baby? On the full moon? Even a blue moon? How long will this journey last?

Some moms enjoy remarkably short stories, an hour or two; other moms work patiently through a slow walk in the park until the baby wriggles his or her way out on the wave of gigantic effort. The shortest labor in my catalog was less than fifteen minutes from beginning to end, no one more shocked that the mom herself. But even the long labors, when the work is finally done, enjoy such relief that the memory of time is suspended, and years later it is hard to accurately recall the progression of minutes and hours.

Were we at the same event, I wonder occasionally, as I hear moms share their birth stories with others? So often the details are wrapped up in attitudes of gratitude, and the hard spots just melt away. What's left is a lovely story, usually of surprise and delight. Our culture likes a bad story, and sometimes moms are thrust into that frame of telling tales one worse than the last. But not with the moms I see. They seem to take the experience as a whole, liking some parts better than others but happy with the result when the ribbons are untied and the delightful package finally gets opened. The newness never gets old; the surprise doesn't dim; the interruption is seldom a bother.

Labors start in the grocery store, standing in line at the bank, in the middle of a movie. Sometimes the rush comes quickly and unexpectedly, like water bursting its dam in the middle of class or ending a sweet dream in the wee hours of the morning or while cooking dinner with company coming in an hour. Priorities change instantly, gratefully, and a new plan takes precedence. *The baby is coming!*

Will she have hair, silken black like her Japanese mother? Will he have downy fur on his shoulders and his back, inviting a kiss to brush your cheeks against? Will his skin be brown, delicious caramel like his grandmother? Or will her hair be fiery red like Grandpa's used to be?

One day I delivered a baby girl with brilliantly reddish locks, almost as if she had been to the beauty parlor. They named her Fiama, Italian for flame, and she fit that description all her days. Her little personality was apparent from the first cry—-lusty and powerful—-and as a little one she stamped her foot once—-well, maybe more than once. Her parents learned to direct that energy in productive and positive ways, but I was always thoroughly amazed and delighted that these gifts of temperament never diminished—just got sent into creative and enriching endeavors.

Now she is a trial attorney in Seattle, and while she no longer stamps her foot, it would indeed be a challenge to be opposite her in a courtroom. What a perfect mystery that unfolded when she came to us. I often get a little hic-cup in my heart when a birth is about to happen, wondering what great surprises are in store for this event and for the future. I never mind the interruption. The anticipation for the package on the other side is far too great.

Though we seldom appreciate the unexpected in other venues, the alteration to the general flow of life presented by a baby is usually entirely acceptable. To halt a conversation mid-sentence, suddenly change long-made plans, cancel a trip within minutes, forego a dinner engagement, or be delighted with an unexpected invitation to "come along"—these experiences, which might seem almost rude in another setting, are thoroughly understood and welcomed when it comes to a baby.

These little one are wrapped in mystery, and every day they delight and surprise us with their smiles, their coos, their beautiful faces that look at us with adoring eyes, their personalities that seem quirky and precious at same time. These babies are divine interruptions, and they make life rich and deep. Who could possibly bring a shift in our lives as perfectly as a baby? Most babies are not planned, and it's lovely that parents have nearly nine months to get used to the idea.

Most of the time we wonder what we could possibly have been thinking, if we'd had any sense, we'd have had these babies a long time ago! That's the ideal, of course. I've found elements of these gracious ideas in every birth experience. Cheryl's birth had all the hallmarks of the birthing business—surprise, interruption, spontaneity, delight, energy, and passion. To be present at the very beginning for that first stupendous breath—the one that starts everything, that sets up the future, and has the capacity to change the world, the breath that seems to rise out of the depths of the sea—-never fails to set me on my heels. It's just gotten better every day.

Risking Life for Life

Would you risk your life for someone you had never met? You might risk your life to save your spouse, certainly to save your child, perhaps even someone you greatly respect and admire or someone who has influenced your life in a significant way. But to purposefully put yourself directly in harm's way for the chance that someone whom you have never met might have life—would you do it? This question presented itself while caring for my friend Laura.

I met Laura several years prior and had the pleasure of catching her second daughter. A delightful woman, full of candor and spontaneity, Laura was completely void of the bitterness or guile that often comes from a difficult upbringing such as hers. Laura loved life, respected her family in spite of thorny issues, and remained determined to rise above the minimal expectations of those around her.

When she came to see me for her first visit in this pregnancy, she was like sunshine bursting through my door. Even though this was an "unexpected" pregnancy, now just five weeks along, Laura made sure to reiterate what I already knew her to believe: that no baby comes by accident. Circumstances may be "sketchy," as she would describe them, but she believed each baby has a God-ordained purpose, and we as parents can elect to sign up or not. Laura, I knew, had already signed on for this new baby with indelible ink.

Just three weeks later, on a soft winter morning, I was very surprised to see her come into my office with an expression I didn't recognize. She was not due to see me for another week, but simply by her countenance—very quiet and somber—I knew she had much to share. As we talked that day, Laura told me a few mornings after our initial meeting she had rolled over in bed to find a painful lump in her right breast. Both her mother and aunt had struggled with the scourge of breast cancer, and Laura sensed immediately that she, too, may have joined their ranks. She promptly saw her physician, and the resulting biopsy confirmed her suspicions. Laura felt as though she were on an emotional pendulum, one moment ecstatic about the news of her pregnancy, then struggling to contain the chocking fingers of fear around her neck.

Because of the aggressive nature of the cancer, Laura was confronted with the ultimate dilemma: terminate the pregnancy in order to undergo a standard cancer-fighting regimen (surgery, chemotherapy, radiation); or risk her life to give her baby a chance. Time was of the essence, and she was advised she needed to act swiftly. Laura shared with me how her extended family and friends, and her physician, counseled her with tenderness and concern for her well-being to choose to end the pregnancy.

"Laura, your life is at stake. Consider terminating this pregnancy. Every day you put this off, every moment you wait to begin treatment; you compromise your chances of survival." Those were heady words indeed. Naturally, Laura was afraid. Only those who have faced this moment and assessed their own mortality can speak about the fear and the challenge that accompany such a situation. She was at a crossroads. Should she take away the chance of life for the baby growing inside her so that she could save her own?

This decision had far-reaching consequences, since Laura had a husband and two other daughters to consider. But the thought of traveling down this wide-open road without her baby was thoroughly unsettling, and she couldn't feel at peace with it. Without any rhyme or reason, Laura just felt that everything would be all right. She had a faith honed by years of difficult experiences. And besides, she was a feisty one!

Laura had many questions and thoughts she shared as we talked but she always came back to her fundamental desire. She just wanted to have her baby and was willing to surrender to the Giver of Life, trusting him to make a way for both her and her baby.

On our next visit, Laura told me she had made up her mind to maintain her pregnancy, and she hoped I would support her decision. I asked her how her husband was doing and what his thoughts were. She told me that, through his tears, he expressed his unwavering support. She was deeply grateful for this token of his regard. I assured her I would stand with her and care for her throughout this pregnancy. She would need to be in close communication with her doctor, as well as an obstetrician, and we would take it one day at a time. She also understood that if she needed to be in a high-risk center for any reason, she would be willing. I could sense the relief she felt after our conversation. Laura knew her decision would be difficult, with lots of unknowns, some discouragements, and pain. It strengthened her to know she had another willing friend to walk alongside her.

First, she proposed to her doctor that they delay any treatment, including the mastectomy, until her pregnancy progressed to the eleventh week. Since she was aware that some pregnancies are lost through natural miscarriage before this pivotal time, she wanted to wait until an ultrasound could confirm if her pregnancy was viable. At that time, she would deal with the breast cancer and whatever recommendations her doctor might suggest. Her doctor agreed to the wait.

The next four to five weeks were intense and full of emotion as Laura and I talked almost daily. Sometimes our conversations would simply be about the weather, a winter storm brewing off the coast that might bring snow and ice or maybe a book she was reading— some light-hearted novel—a way to pass the time. Sometimes we talked about her two little girls: Kari, a bright and cheery four-year-old, whose words seemed to tumble out of her mouth like handfuls of the sweetest peppermint taffy; and Mina, a precocious two-year-old, with golden curls cascading down her forehead when she bent down to play with the toys in my waiting room.

How Laura longed for them to have a good life, to watch them grow to be loving, kind, tenderhearted women of courage and purpose. Laura was teaching them well, I could see, and they were a delight to have around. Their giggles made everyone turn and smile, such pure joy and innocence. Of course, their natural mischief played out at these visits as well and provided the welcome laughter we all needed. Their little minds loved organization, and the basket of small plastic animals, sea creatures, mammals, snakes, and frogs would end up all in a row: yellow ones in a line, green ones by themselves, tall ones in the back, fat ones in the middle, horses standing alone. Noah's ark of pairs all together. I'm always amazed to watch these little geniuses at play; they're so small, but they know so much! It was a good time, and I lingered over these visits.

Time moved slowly along the calendar that month; morning and night stretched to prolong the bliss of ignorance while still feeling the quiet trepidation. Finally, at the eleven-week mark, Laura's ultrasound confirmed a strong heartbeat and excellent growth—the expectation for a normal baby. Laura and her husband were thrilled.

Now, with a vision of this wonderful addition to her family, she was ready to have a conversation with her most kind physician about the next step to deal with the breast cancer: surgery. In this discussion, she asked for one more thing. Laura elected to undergo the mastectomy with as minimal anesthesia as possible. She wanted the smallest exposure to the growing baby in her womb. Laura's courage could be felt, and I was touched to the core by her sacrifice and deep expression of love for this little baby.

Her surgery went well, and after a period of weeks for recovery, Laura began chemotherapy. She was placed on a regimen of treatment considered safe for an unborn baby. This allowed Laura to go through the remainder of her pregnancy as strong and ready for a healthy labor as possible. Once the baby was born, she would undergo further tests and radiation as indicated.

Walking alongside this lovely woman was quite emotional. At every appointment, Laura came in with a positive attitude and an inner strength fueled by her passion to look in her baby's eyes, kiss that little rosebud of a mouth, and feel a little heartbeat against her bare chest. Knowing what she would be facing, now and in the months to come, did not produce the discouragement I thought might arise. She considered her chances of living a long life might not be terrific, but she refused to become disheartened and chose to treasure every single day. She neither regretted the decisions she made nor allowed herself to give in to the feelings of fear that must have been pounding on the doors of her spirit.

Laura kept an open and brave mind, and her forthrightness held her in good stead as she dealt daily with these matters. She came to rely increasingly on her supportive husband and her friends. It was greatly reassuring when the baby began to kick every day; that confirmation of life was so uplifting. During her trial, Laura had several angels who helped her with her little girls when she needed rest.

These friends brought meals, flowers, and notes of encouragement; they showed up to do a load of laundry, to pick up groceries, to bring their children to play with hers on occasion, appearing always in moments of crisis to soften the blow. Laura never needed to stand alone or consider her request for help to be a burden. Her community was blessed to care for its wounded, and Laura was ever grateful. Her periodic ultrasounds revealed normal growth and a girl baby! Laura was especially thrilled to think that these sisters would always have each other to lean on.

Near the end of her pregnancy, Laura continued to see her physician and me. She was doing well, the baby was growing normally, and she was beginning to feel those Braxton Hicks contractions so common toward the finish line. She was released to my care for the birth, so we began to make preparations for the big event. Her two sisters made batches of sugar cookies with candy sprinkles, Laura's favorite.

Her two daughters drew pictures of what their new sister might look like, giving her jumbles of yellow hair and bright red lips. Of course, her eyes were blue. These sweet pictures decorated the cabinets, the refrigerator, the doors (on both sides), with a few extra on the table for good measure. Laura was gratified with this attention, which made the coming day so much more special. Her husband had gathered some flowers from an organic field near their house: pink peonies, purple irises, yellow and orange day lilies, and a few white carnations——an assortment of colors and textures that made Laura smile. Clearly the waiting had begun.

As June slipped in to July, I listened for The Phone Call, announcing the impending arrival of this little girl. July third became July fourth, with occasional fireworks lighting the midnight sky in anticipation of the afternoon's celebration all over the lake. Laura called and said simply, "We'll be on our way in just a few moments. Contractions began about an hour ago, and now they're four minutes apart." Laura and her husband, two sisters, and her daughters, arrived about 4:00 a.m. There were flowers on the desk, candy in a bowl, cookies on a decorated plate. I could see that this was going to be a celebration. Sporadic fireworks added their pop and bang while Laura labored.

The labor was not long, and not difficult, which is the nice thing about Baby Number Three. Each contraction brought her just micrometers closer, like getting up in the morning and tiptoeing down one stair at a time to open presents that have been waiting nine whole months. The anticipation was delicious, and the work of labor added to the sweetness. When this baby was born, four hours later, the entire room erupted in tears. We were all awash with the dew of heaven! For the whole family, who had journeyed together through many tough months, this was truly a day to rejoice.

This little baby was so welcomed, after such an ordeal, that the family felt it as their own private Independence Day. They named her Phoebe June, but her sisters called her "Pretty Jane." I always remember the look on Laura's face and the tears in her eyes as she gazed at the daughter she risked so much to meet. And what a beauty she was——round cherubic face, blue eyes, perfectly pink body. She looked just like the pictures Kari and Mina had drawn. All she needed was some glitter glam on her cheeks!

For several years I kept in touch with Laura and her family, seeing her at the breast cancer walk each summer. She had further treatment and radiation following the birth of Pretty Jane, and to my knowledge, she remained clear of cancer by the four-year mark. She has since moved, and we have lost contract. I was humbled by her courage and her passion for life, even if it meant the possibility of losing her own. In our society, few would have faulted Laura had she chosen otherwise and walked a different path; but Laura chose life. I feel confident that Phoebe is ever grateful for such unconditional love. I pray that God's plan for this sweet baby brings joy and gladness, because it was always clear that her mother had surely signed on—heart and soul!

The Beauty and the Birth

Lakewold Gardens is a magnificent, historic, ten-acre estate located just outside the city of Tacoma, Washington. It offers a breathtaking tourist experience with its Georgian-style mansion surrounded by extensive acreage consisting of landscape architecture by Thomas Church, regal statuaries, and exquisite garden rooms of rare plants and native foliage. Lakewold Gardens is situated to capture incredible panoramic views of both Mount Rainier and Gravelly Lake, with the expanse of Puget Sound in the distance. Because of its incredible beauty, these gardens have been a popular location for weddings, outdoor symphonies, and other large celebrations for almost one hundred years. For Ruth and Danny, this was the perfect place to birth a baby. As caretakers of the mansion at Lakewold Gardens, Ruth and Danny lived in a wonderfully quaint apartment adjacent to the home's south wing. Outfitted with traditional radiator pipes and old-fashioned wood trim in every room, their apartment was small in comparison to the mansion, but very unique and nostalgic.

In addition, the scenery they enjoyed daily, each season more beautiful than the last, compensated entirely for the modest square footage of their residence. Ruth had delivered her first child with me just one year earlier, a handsome and gregarious boy, Antonio, with masses of black wavy hair shadowing big brown eyes. He was just too cute! Ruth and I had become good friends. I was looking forward to Ruth's delivery date with great anticipation.

Spring was in full bloom, and the gardens were especially resplendent. It was Antonio's first birthday, and Ruth and Danny had planned a first birthday party with all the trimmings. There were party favors, decorative hats, confetti, and banners, a full-course barbeque, and a very large bunch of multi-colored balloons to be released after cake and ice cream.

So when I received Ruth's call on that splendid spring morning, informing me her labor had begun, I laughed out loud. How perfect! Such an event, within-an-event, to grace historic Lakewold Gardens!

As I neared the Gardens, I drove through massive, hundred-year-old maple and elm trees, up toward the graceful mansion with its stately columns and brick walkways, edged by dense hedges of green. Azaleas of magenta and purple and pink bloomed brightly, and pine boughs brushed the car as the wheels made a soft crunching sound on the gravel, reminding me of the rose gardens behind my grandparents' home in Santa Monica when I was four years old.

I was immediately transported to hear robins and wrens splashing in the bird bath, the heady smell of red roses, and the sound of my little shoes on the gravel walkway, more than 60 years before. As I finished my reverie, I wondered who else might have been born in this splendid place. What effects had its walls and halls and paintings and statues had on a small child, looking up at all the Big People while he held his Papa's hand ever so tightly?

While I enjoyed this pleasant remembrance, I unloaded my car to the fragrance of roses and rhododendrons and walked up to the house with the sound of pea gravel and pine needles crackling underfoot. As I rounded the corner to their apartment, I was greeted by the sight of children in party hats running amidst birthday balloons, and Danny waving at me from the balcony as he stood grilling hamburgers and hot dogs for the guests. What a celebratory environment.

I walked into their house to find Ruth in the kitchen, still enjoying the early rumblings of labor, excited about the events about to unfold on this wonderful day. The baby seemed to be quite content for the moment, with excellent heart tones, ready to make his streak toward the light in the coming hours. Soon her contractions began to pinch a bit, so Ruth decided to hand out the party favors to the children, serve the cake and ice cream, release the bundle of balloons, and say a happy and excited "good-bye" to the guests.

Ruth's birth was serene that day, just like a lovely melody, a few crescendos culminating in a burst of sweat and power, followed by a lingering pause. Outside the window, the reflection of the swans on the pond below in the gardens presented an almost dreamy effect. In early labor, Ruth recalled later, the rise and fall of her contractions reminded her of waves rippling to the shore beyond the big trees overlooking the Sound. The rhythm was sure but gentle. In the next few hours, Ruth's labor pains increased, gradually at first, then with might, like the unrelenting hammer stroke of a powerful machine. She turned quiet, with an air of silent anticipation. Conversation ceased, a respectful distance creating an aura around her of intense, other-worldly expectation. Then the labor shifted, almost suddenly, into a higher octave, and she made those guttural, hard-working noises that signal the final push to birth. Within just a few moments, Matteo was born with a shock of black hair on his head, and on his ears, on his shoulders, and on his arms a soft downy fur so light and beautiful. *What a gorgeous baby, I thought, with a perfect mama and such a supportive, loving papa.*

With the house already festooned with balloons and party decorations, it was a seamless transition from one celebration to the next. The photos taken from the birth were delightful: Antonio, a vivacious one-year-old, and Matteo only one hour old but already showing his brother's sparkle to be invited to the party. After everything settled down, Matteo was "snuzzled" next to his mom, nursing vigorously, and we all sat together to enjoy delicious leftover hamburgers, birthday cake, and ice cream.

In the waning hours of the evening, with dusk falling softly through the tall trees and evergreens, I said my goodbyes and began my drive home from this birth. The last glow of sunset was quickly fading to the blue-black of night, and a few stars were twinkling overhead. This day was filled with good humor, a bit of hard work, family, and friends to welcome a new life, all while celebrating the one-year anniversary of another. It was a day of pure joy. I thought, *Every baby should be welcomed in such a festive way!*

The next morning after my experience at Lakewold Gardens, I received a call from Holly, another mom-to-be. She was sure she was in labor, so I verified the driving directions with her husband, Rick, promptly packed up my newly sterilized instruments into my birth bag, and set out for her home. I carefully followed Rick's map and, in the end, found myself in the middle of a highly industrial area of town, a separate world from the greenery of the day before. I felt a bit puzzled, as there were no houses anywhere around.

I stopped at the proper address, and checked my map to see if perhaps I had misunderstood Rick's directions. I was in front of a machine shop with no apparent access on the main road. Just then, Rick appeared around the corner, breathless with excitement, and instructed me to pull around to the rear of the shop. I met him in the back of what I later learned was the machine shop where he worked, and turned left to find Holly thick in labor.

The space was small and compact, like a big hug on this early spring day, and there was a nice, cool breeze coming in from all the open windows. This was Rick and Holly's first child, and I could sense the tremendous anticipation and excitement both were feeling. It was beautiful to witness how gentle and attentive Rick was to his wife. He was willing to do anything to make her comfortable, never leaving her side and catering to her every need. I could see from his expression that it was hard for him to watch her labor, unable to ameliorate her pain but relieved with the passing of each contraction. Holly, like many women, was focused inward and spoke little. But she hummed a few bars of a soft melody at the end of each contraction, as if the song would eventually take flight and at its end she would find the baby.

By mid-afternoon, Holly was clearly ready for this baby to come, and with renewed energy and power, she gathered up her determination and birthed her lovely baby into the waiting hands of her sweet husband. Tears of joy and relief enveloped them both, like the rainbow after a storm splashes through. The love they shared was so tangible, and the words they exchanged over their beautiful child were tender and affectionate. I stepped back to offer them as much privacy as I could, quietly pulling the curtain across the bed.

The atmosphere was magical within this bus-turned-home. So beautiful was their embracing of their new baby, so exquisite their loving glances into each other's eyes, as if all the flowers of Lakewold Gardens had replaced the sea of brick and concrete outside and suddenly blossomed inside this small enclosure, suffusing the air with all their fragrance and beauty. I recalled my musing of last evening, *Every baby's birth is such miraculous event, and every child should be welcomed with festivities and balloons and fireworks.*

Holly's birth reminded me that true beauty is nurtured in the gardens of the soul. Holly and Rick surrounded their baby with all the party decorations that matter: sparklers of joy, ribbons of happiness, and confetti of delight.

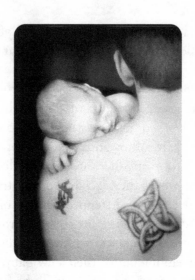

The Pirate Husband

Ching ching. It was gorgeous, sunny spring morning in the Pacific Northwest—the perfect day for a baby to be born. The sun was shining, it was not too hot, and a refreshing cool breeze was drifting off the Puget Sound. *Ching ching.* Mary Jane was laboring beautifully, and everything was progressing evenly and quietly. This was her third baby, she knew what her internal rhythm needed to be, and she was dancing to the music easily. *Ching ching.* The only thing about this birth that was out of the ordinary was that peculiar metallic clicking sound coming from the kitchen. I was very curious about the source of it, but I wanted to spend some time with Mary Jane. I would get to kitchen soon enough I smiled to myself because I knew that her husband, Clive, must be up to something unique…

From the day this eclectic couple entered my birth center, I knew we were going to have an adventure. Creatively dressed for our first visit in an earthy, ample, long muslin skirt, with patches of purple tie-dye embroidered here and there around the hem,

Mary Jane was simply bubbling with the excitement of her third pregnancy. Her long braid was tied down her back with a handful of yellow yarn bundled up to make a splash of color against her lacy blue overshirt. And Clive, hair slightly askew even when dressed for business, was beaming with pride at the thought of becoming a father to another precious baby. He smiled through his not-too-manicured goatee as he spoke of his anticipation. Every appointment with them at the birth center was a delight as we visited about daily life and their latest caper. Both viewed life with a creative flair, and I thoroughly enjoyed their sense of freedom from ordinary social customs.

On the day of the birth, the trip to their home took about an hour. It was a lovely drive through winding roads and past large tracts of land shadowed by huge evergreen trees. The sunlight intersected the black branches of these giants of trees and shone on the cushy blanket of pine, hemlock and yew needles below. The air smelled fresh and clean after the previous evening showers, scrubbed and crisp to welcome this new being about to be born. At the end of the road, the landscape opened suddenly to a large expanse of sea—the Puget Sound. The waves lapped the shore and splashed against the sides of the small, three-car ferryboat waiting to transport me across.

So much beauty surrounded me in this little bit of paradise. The breeze that accompanied this brief ferry escort to Herron Island felt dreamy on my skin, like a gauzy shawl tickling my arms. I approached their home with a sense of expectancy and excitement. I prayed that this baby would be able to enjoy many moments like this one, and I thanked God for such a beautiful setting.

When I arrived at their door, Clive, with his black hair disheveled and boots untied, met me and took me straight to the bedroom where Mary Jane was pacing purposefully around the wide bed. She was dressed in a colorful skirt—another dyed muslin of blues and greens—and her fully belly just barely peeked out from under her stretched white cotton top. She looked like a spring bouquet as she swayed to the rise and fall of each contraction. It is such a special pleasure to be in someone's home for the unfolding of this miracle; a family's personality and endearing quirkiness sits on every shelf and camps in every corner.

Theirs was a rustic little house, a cottage really, with a picket fence, goats in the back, chickens in the roost, and happy golden retriever with a whapping tail to greet visitors at the door. Their early-depression house, build in the late 1930's, was made of logs felt nearby and chinked ever so carefully to keep out the draft; it fell homey and safe. A fire smoldered in the stone fireplace, river rock framing the large opening for logs of noble fir and pine. It warmed the edges of this spring day and brought comfort and cheer. An old cast-iron teapot hung on a metal bar above the embers, and I could smell the fragrant odor of chamomile brewing as I walked back to the bedroom at the end of the short hallway.

I was anxious to listen to their little baby, to be comforted by the sound of his heart. The steady thump-thump always settled on the ears like the refrain of a favorite love song. So while Mary Jane focused inwardly on her labor, on the movement of her baby and the birth soon to come, I began to unload my midwifery supplies. As I was doing so, I was surprised to hear a distinctive *ching ching* coming from the kitchen. Any other time I would have let my mind wander through the possibilities of what that repetitive sound could be; but at the moment, I had a job to do.

After setting up my birth bag and making sure Mary Jane was safe and happy, I listened to the baby. He reached out to me with a loud and steady "beat, beat, beat" on my hand-held doppler. What a glorious sound! Everything taken care of for the moment, I wandered into the kitchen to get Mary Jane some juice and an apple. Through the picture window, I could see two sailboats playing into the wind and a kayak cutting the water silently and swiftly on this secluded portion of the Sound. *Ching ching*…where was that clinking coming from?

I looked around to see Clive sitting at their kitchen table, and on the floor next to him was a large mound of quarters! Like a pirate counting his booty, he was piling heaps of quarters onto the wooden table, carefully counting out the silvers, and—*ching ching ching*— dropping them into one of two large canvas bags open on the floor. Just then, Mary Jane peeked out of the bedroom door to smile at him, reassuring him that she was doing just fine. I was amused and only a tiny bit surprised that she seemed oblivious to her Long John Silver husband, as if this were quite a common occurrence.

Clive looked up at me and laughed. "Oh...I don't like dealing with paper money. I handle all my business affairs this way. Do you mind if I pay you in quarters?"

"Clive, I would expect nothing less from you," I said with a smile. "Whatever denomination suits you, suits me"

Mary Jane's labor progressed quickly, and the birth of their precious little boy came just as the sun was setting over the spectacular Olympic Mountains in the distance. Clive and Mary Jane were as pleased as punch. After welcoming and smothering their new baby with hugs and kisses, Clive brought from the kitchen a veritable gourmet snack with delicacies the sea so richly provides. He had neatly arranged on a platter some smoked salmon—which he had caught himself and prepared in his trusty Indian Smoker—some halibut cheeks, assorted crackers with Gouda, Swiss, cheddar, and havarti cheeses. He had decorated the platter with some seaweed, parsley, and chives. In a pot on the stove, I could smell corn and clam chowder. Did he think we were having party? He offered his favorite Chablis wine and some sparkling white grape juice.

Together we toasted the beauty of the baby and the birth and the day. We reveled in the smell of that newborn and laughed at his sweet little cry. Why do they always sound like little lambs? He nursed for a long time, almost two hours. Already he was such an expert. Gradually, the darkening of the night sky enveloped land and sea, and the first stars began to peep out. It was time for me to go.

I packed up my midwife's suitcase and began to say my good-byes. Clive got up and heaved the two canvas bags from the kitchen onto his shoulders. Each was loaded with quarters like booty from the depths of the ocean, and he plunked them into the trunk of my little red Datsun. I laughed as the weight of silvers visibly lowered the back end of my car.

The voyage across the Sound on that tiny ferry was absolutely refreshing, and it gave me time to file away this wonderful day into the memory of my heart. The entire experience, down to the bags of quarters, endeared me to this couple more than ever. They were a fresh reminder how crucial humor and a light-hearted approach to life are to this otherwise very serious business of living. They had liberated themselves from the pressures of conformity and gave each other the room to express their individualities. And in this freedom, they lived a thoroughly spontaneous, happy life.

What a funny finale to a great birth. I think of Clive and Mary Jane whenever I drive that lovely, lonely road out to the end of the Sound; and in my mind's eye, I imagine a pirate ship called the *HMS Mary Jane* captained by Long Clive Silver counting out his quarters…

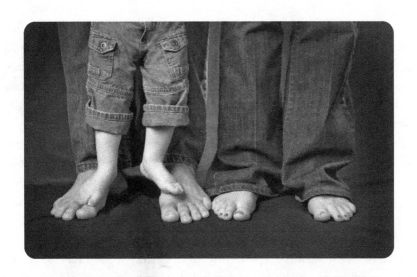

Timing Is Everything

The life of a midwife is certainly interesting: odd hours, frequent interruptions, never knowing from day to day what's about to happen, and of course, miracles daily. There are a few minor occupational details that come into play. I seldom go outside pager range; I rarely go camping with my family; and my husband and I take two cars nearly everywhere we go. We're occasionally interrupted at a restaurant, and I'm out the door for another great adventure, while he's left with the bill.

One Sunday afternoon we had tickets to see Andrew Lloyd Webber's *The Phantom of the Opera.* We usually don't go to plays, as the disruption of a call, even on silent/vibrate mode, might be bothersome to other patrons, but we thought we might take a chance with this one. As we were traveling up Interstate 5—in separate cars, of course—and sure enough my pager rang, and I signaled my husband that he should go on without me. I took the next exit off I-5, turned around, and shortly arrived at Cathy's home.

She was laboring nicely, with contractions now about five minutes apart. We had time to talk about her two children, five and three, who were at grandma's playing in the backyard. She knew they would be "in her lap" during labor, so having them close but not in the middle of things seemed the best course. Her husband, Arnie, put on some music—favorite songs he knew Cathy would like— nothing too loud or too persistent, just some soft background noises that softened the thunder occurring inside her. She got into the tub for an hour, which felt so relaxing, then got out again.

Water is such comfort, especially during labor; sometimes moms just don't want to get out, and the baby gets born there. But Cathy liked her bleached white sheets, hung outside in the breeze the day before, smelling so fresh and clean. With everything set up, we patiently waited for this baby to announce his impending arrival. Not too long after, Cathy declared, "Let's roll." Such a funny expression but exactly Cathy-like. She got up into her big four-poster bed, settled into the sheets just so, and pushed out her shiny, wriggly baby boy, all seven pounds and thirteen ounces of him. He had bright orange hair, just like his mom and his siblings. What could have been better than that! This was opera, play and performance all wrapped up together with bright ribbons.

I never regretted for a moment missing the play; however, by happenstance, I was about to have a second chance. The next day my brother from Iowa came into town for a visit. I had not seen him for about five years, so we talked and talked. In response to his question about how our lives accommodated midwifery, I told him the story about "disappearing" and leaving my husband to go to the opera alone. He looked at me and said, "Well, my best friend, Rick, is currently playing the Phantom!" And with that, he picked up the phone, called his actor friend at the Sheraton Hotel in Seattle, who secured two seats directly under the chandelier at the Paramount Theatre for us for the next day. And what a performance it was, absolutely incredible, with no pager interruptions. It felt like a blessing for all the "missing," and we enjoyed every moment.

I have to admit, however, that I did not start out to engage in a life of midwifery. Many moons ago, when I attended the University of Washington, I planned to be a French correspondent, perhaps even an interpreter at the United Nations, with trips across the pond from time to time, lunch at the Eiffel Tower, and frequent visits to the D'Orsay Museum. As a seventeen-year-old I envisioned a romantic life dashing about the world, speaking foreign languages with ease, visiting idyllic hideaways and exotic lands. In my imagination, I could smell the lavender fields, taste the rich cheeses and French pastries (that I'm still drawn to), and feel the soothing breezes off the coast of Southern France as I looked with fairy eyes on the Mediterranean. Young dreams are sweet. However, reality edged its way in as I approached twenty, and I switched majors at the end, graduating with a Bachelors of Arts in English literature. My honors thesis was about childbirth in literature—clearly the compass was beginning to turn, even before I understood entirely that a much better life awaited me down the road.

Now years later as a midwife, my occupation is quite different from the romanticism of a French correspondent. But while the boundaries of my life are clear and tight; the boundaries of my heart have remained endless. I follow my babies all over the world and live vicariously through their splendid experiences. And even here at home, from time to time life has offered some delicious surprises.

Evelyn and Tom lived on Anderson Island, just off the shores of Steilacoom, in the lovely Puget Sound area south of Tacoma. The only access to this idyll is a ferryboat that lumbers back and forth during the daylight hours, concluding its final passage about seven o'clock in the evening. A large lake sits in the middle of this forested refuge, which is otherwise surrounded with ocean waters that lap at its shoreline with the rising and falling tides. Those who are blessed to live there cherish its privacy, its protection, and its unparalleled beauty. They revel in the "inconvenience" of the ferry traffic, as it keeps travelers away. Life is unhurried, a throwback to the era of small towns with single grocery marts, friendly gas station clerks, bankers who know your names as well as the names of your children, and neighbors who are untroubled by a midnight call for assistance.

Evelyn had delivered two babies on the mainland with me, lovely little sweet peas, whose eyes sparkled like stars in the night sky, with rosy cheeks and fat little fingers and toes. She and Tom had come late to the rush of babies and now were making up for lost time with number four on the way in five years.

Their large, sprawling home looked down across a broad expanse of meadow and through some old-growth fir trees to the Sound. Chickens and goats occupied the upper portion of this twenty-acre parcel, with a vegetable garden stuck in between the rabbit hutches and the horse barn on the easterly slope. Sunshine filtered through some pine trees farther down, revealing massive rhododendron flowers in pinks and purples, azaleas peeking up here and there, an air of calm pervading.

Tom was a retired concrete engineer, and his house was constructed entirely of concrete—even the roof. In the late spring, handfuls of flower seeds would be thrown up onto its dirt-strewn top, growing up into masses of wild flowers in shades of orange, pink, red, white, and yellow. It looked quite a bit like an old woman's straw hat, with pieces of hay stuck at odd angles, ribbons curling down along the side, a burst of color all around the edges. Inside the house, the children romped and played, banging the screen door as they rushed inside, outside, and around the pump house in a game of "catch me if you can."

I knew Evelyn was approaching her day to deliver. She hung over the bed frame more often now to take in deep breaths, holding a hand against her swelling belly to feel those kicks and jabs. She knew she would soon miss that lovely movement inside, but oh, how wonderful to get her body back. Her legs ached by the end of the day, and her pelvis felt full and tight as the baby rolled from side to side. She had two weeks to go and had seen me in my office only the day before. Her cervix wasn't ready yet, but she told me she thought that might change quickly, at least it felt like it would. She was beginning to sense some "pinching," and her uterus would often ball up hard, like the skin of a taut basketball.

After dinner, the children hustled up to bed as the sun set beyond the horizon. Evelyn was tired too and soon pushed herself into the oversized bed she had inherited from her grandfather. She had to climb up into this massive bed on steps Tom had made her, and once there, she was reluctant to get out.

At 2:15 a.m., Evelyn awoke to the definitive sensation that the baby wanted out. Evelyn knew she was late in the game, having probably contracted in her sleep during the last few hours, as she was so tired. She knew there wasn't much time. The ferry boat on and off the island didn't run at night, and the only way to get to the mainland was by emergency air rescue. Evelyn awoke Tom, and then they called me. I quickly told them I would come down to the Steilacoom dock, while they made arrangements as they could, we would keep in touch by cell phone.

Within forty minutes, I was parked at the dock, noticing only a few cars that remained overnight, and already their windshields were covered with a 3:00 a.m. mist. A long train carrying freight to far off places rumbled past some minutes after as I crossed the tracks, making its mournful wail as it passed me at forty miles per hour. Standing on the dock with my suitcase and oxygen tank, I must have appeared a strange sight to the engineer. He peered curiously through the window of his locomotive as he rushed by.

Soon quiet engulfed the air, and the only sound came from small waves along the boat ramp. The ferry ticket booth was closed for the night, a single light bulb illuminating the path in front. In the distance, I could see a few scattered boats; their lights reflected like a painter's stroke in the undulating waters of the Sound. A new noise rose, soft at first, then louder as it came near. The sound of the tiny motor grew until I could pinpoint the source, a small boat trolling toward the landing. This craft, not much bigger than a rowboat, presented itself as the relief vehicle to take me to Evelyn and Tom's. It appeared that they had decided against the air rescue. A kindly older man, their nearest neighbor, had agreed to play the gentle hero, launching into the dark to meet me. He put my suitcase and oxygen tank in the bottom, invited me to jump in, and soon we were speeding around the island to a private dock nearer Evelyn's home. A car was waiting there, and with a few words and gestures, I was escorted into the back seat, whisked away to Evelyn's, and deposited in their long, circuitous driveway.

Tom came out, helping me and my things into the house and upstairs, where Evelyn was happily ensconced in the bed, her smiling face glistening with the effort of labor, clearly getting ready to welcome her baby into the world. Evelyn shushed everyone quiet, breathed through several contractions, sighed her relief at the end, and waited for the unmistakable signal to push. She wanted to let this baby slide right out, so she withheld that powerful urge just before baby comes. She breathed in measured cadences, counting to thirty, then took a deep breath and settled into her overstuffed pillows. After perhaps ten of these cycles, she felt her baby with the next contraction nearly exit the doorway. So she gave a little push, and soon this perfectly round head with little tufts of brown hair appeared, quickly followed by arms and legs, fingers, toes, and a sweet cry. Marya slid into her daddy's arms just at the first faint light of the morning.

Within minutes, Marya was nuzzled in her mother's arms, nursing hungrily. It was only after this flurry of strange, hurried activity that I was able to stop, take in a deep breath, and thank God that every moment had worked out well, and mom and baby were safe and happy.

As I was leaving a few hours later, already it was clear that it would surely be another lovely day. Star lights began to fade, and house lights started to take their place, twinkling on here and there. A line of cars formed along the southern side of the meadow, peeking through the trees, the still sleepy drivers holding steaming mugs of coffee, bunching up like bumper cars for the first ferry of the morning to take them to Tacoma. What had they all unknowingly missed in the night? A new member of their small community's family!

While anything French is a distant memory now, I'm in the best space of all, keeping a journal of adventures, each birth a unique event full of emotion, passion, power, and strength. No spy on a covert mission could have as many surprises as I; no one with plans perfectly designed and executed could enjoy the spontaneity I have. There is more wonder in this occupation than anyone could order up, even with the most intricate planning. Without a schedule, still everything happens just as it should and on time. In this arena, timing indeed is everything.

Home Is Where the Horns Are

Home is where the heart is. This saying is certainly a much-used cliché, but its truth remains. Many of my patients choose to deliver their babies in the coziness and comfort of their own homes. It's a delight to enter their "heart-lodges" for one of the most significant and a wonderful events of their lives; and every encounter is precious. There just is no substitute for the intimacy shared in someone else's home.

So much is discovered about a person simply by exploring the well—thought -out details of a home—the colors chosen, the strategic placement of furniture, the small treasures proudly displayed as mementos of special events. For some, there is an explosion of intense colors in every room, sometimes highlighted by wall art of all genres. Others prefer a home carefully and pristinely organized in mono-chromatic palates with minimal decor. One appears serene and peaceful; another shouts with vibrancy and verve. The uniqueness and variety of personalities find expression in the details of the home's environment. *Vive la Difference!*

The home is an extension of the heart and soul, so I look forward to whatever I encounter. Even the exquisite aromas of a household attach themselves to a person, and after months of meeting in my office, there are times I could recognize the patient's identity simply by the cheery smell of their home.

But on one occasion, I was quite surprised when I walked into a home. Jerry and Ellen were natives of Alaska and had moved to the Puget Sound area for job relocation. Although they had lived in the Seattle area for quite some time, they still carried the robust, pioneer spirit of a true Alaskan...especially Jerry. While Ellen had a very feminine quality with hints of urban influence, Jerry was a frontiersman through and through. Consistently clad in flannel plaid and burly boots, this rough-hewn man with several days' growth of beard filled a room with his hearty voice and infectious laughter. He prided himself on being a skilled hunter with gun and bow, and any leave of absence from his job designing machinery for a cabinet factory found him out in the open air, ready to overtake his prey.

Usually it is the woman who has full custodial rights to the house's decor. Most men leave the decorating to the woman, understanding the meaning of the well-worn cliché. *If mama ain't happy...ain't nobody happy!* Besides, as long as his personal needs are satisfied and there's food on the table, most men are content with the atmosphere in the home their wife creates. He may actually enjoy seeing what she produces with her crafts or her artist's eye or her skill at collecting. In this house, however, Jerry certainly set the tone and created the ambiance!

When I initially parked my car outside their home on the day of their first child's birth, I took in a sight I very much expected from this Alaskan couple. Their home was nestled among many very old pine trees, and I felt as if I had entered a vacation lodge secluded from civilization. I walked up to the log cabin, crunching pinecones with every step and smelling the wonderfully crisp mountain air very common to this region. Jerry opened the big wooden door, with its cast iron knocker in the shape of elk's antlers, welcoming me with anticipation. It was what greeted me next that made me laugh.

When he moved aside to escort me inside the lodge, I came face-to-face with an enormous moose head! Incredibly furry and lifelike as he stared into my eyes, I half expected to feel his hot breath on my cheek as I passed him by. Seeing my amused expression, Jerry exclaimed, "Yes! Meet Max the Moose. He's one of my very first exploits. Come in and meet the rest!" *The rest?* I thought.

I turned the corner of the entryway into the expansive great-room of this lodge and was arrested by the sight of many horns pointing; it seemed, in every direction. Curly horns of goats, straight horns of antelopes, curved tusks of boars, antlers of every variety, shape, and size…Everywhere I looked my eyes landed upon some type of bone or cartilage extending from the wall. As my eyes adjusted to this maze of protrusions, I was able to take in the full picture as the animal heads attached to those horns made themselves known. It seemed all available wall space was inhabited by the head of a creature, once living, now expertly stuffed and mounted; in the corners stood full-bodied animals in lifelike poses. They seemed ready to pounce, to run, or to charge full on. I marveled at the amazing expression this room provided.

"Well, what do you think?" asked Jerry of his bold display of hunting and taxidermy skill.

"Truly amazing!" I exclaimed.

Just then I heard Ellen's soft greeting. She had been standing there, waiting for the introduction to conclude, and I could see the humor and delight in her eyes. Just as she adored the man she married, she treasured the extension of his personality tangibly exhibited throughout their home. In addition, it was evident she was completely at peace within her masculine surroundings as she spent the next hours laboring. How delicately and artfully she waltzed through the maze of horns, dancing through the beautiful rhythm of birthing their first child. She filled the space with her femininity, while dodging the lifelike displays as she walked the labor path around and round in her home.

Jerry and Ellen brought forth all three of their children inside that lodge, underneath the mass of horns, and every visit to their home was as delightful as the first. They have since moved back to their native state of Alaska, and I often entertain myself with visions of both their boys and girl, and the children they have since had, embracing the passions of their father and living out the thrilling pursuit of the hunt...There will, of course, need a much larger lodge!

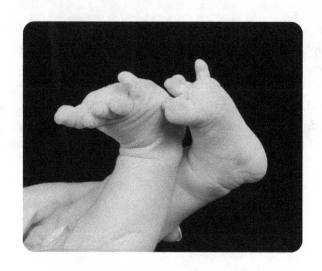

An Ultrasound Paints 1,000 Words

Ultrasound technology has been the single most important invention with regards to the preservation of an unborn baby's life. Offering a visual image of a rapidly beating heart at a mere seven weeks pregnant and pairs of beautifully tiny arms and legs at eleven weeks; watching thrilling kicking and punching movements seen, but not yet felt, at thirteen weeks; it can transfix a newly pregnant couple. It gives them an opportunity to understand and connect with the treasure growing inside.

Ultrasound pictures possess great power, supplying tangible evidence of the life that begins at conception. Gentle terms come to mind, describing the barest beginnings of life as the event when "the sperm and egg meet in the hallways, kiss, and walk down the aisle." My moms and dads understand that "this little pencil dot grows into a small pea, into a robust lima bean, into a flittering flutter bug, into a kicking puppy, into a sweet pumpkin pie, into a baby!"—-and comes out looking just like you!

We have all sorts of affectionate phrases and terms for our babies, sometimes labeling our children far into adulthood with these aphorisms. They are salient credit to the sure, instinctive awareness that babies are babies are babies, from the first shot out of the barn. What may once have been considered only a bunch of cells can now be clearly seen as a precious child, awaiting the chance to fulfill a God-given destiny in the world. Ultrasound has provided voice and visions to that certain knowledge and can be credited as a true life-saving tool.

Helping a couple see a first glimpse of their baby is one of my most exciting moments. This amazing "photo-op" has never become anything less than spectacular. Tears all around are the common reaction. It is gratifying to hear, "I never knew," or "I had no idea they were so well-formed," or "Hey, he has your nose, John!" Often there are sudden tears, sometimes a real belly laugh, occasionally the silence of awe or surprise or shock or wonderment; priceless expressions. Such pictures usually firm a woman's resolve to bring this child safety and happily into the world. Perhaps especially rewarding, these ultrasound pictures often help to bring clarity to a young woman overwhelmed at the confirmation of an unexpected pregnancy. They can help her define the last few days or weeks of personal upheaval and encourage her to make some very important decisions.

That leap into adulthood happens, sometimes, in the moment it takes for the ultrasound unit to warm up. Like turning on a machine, these ob scans can fire up a young person's movement into maturity, transporting carefree youth into the sobering realm of adulthood. Yesterday, a young girl was making decisions about whether to go shopping Friday night or instead to enjoy pizza and a movie with some friends. Today she is confronted with the choice of facing her parents with the announcement of an unplanned pregnancy or somehow privately finding a way to abort the life within her. She may feel completely overwhelmed with too many options and none.

Tina had been to the birth of her friend Amy's baby nearly a year before. I remembered Tina as a sweet girl with wavy brown hair caught up in a ponytail, wearing jeans and a sweatshirt. She was sixteen at the time, on the verge of adulthood but still enjoying teenage music and style, care-free, and beginning to assume some independence in her life. She was happy for her friend but clearly certain that she was not ready yet for that experience! Her parents were going through a separation, and while Amy labored, Tina and I talked a little about how hard this was for her. She just didn't understand but was glad the endless arguments would cease. She looked forward to a more peaceful time and had a new boyfriend, Gene, whom she liked a lot.

Almost a year had elapsed, like the quick flickering of a light, and Tina was in my office now with tears and fear. At seventeen, she was still a young girl but no longer so carefree. She told me she had missed two periods and just had a positive pregnancy test. It was clear that what she needed most was good information and loving support.

Tina and I spent quite a while discussing what her options were. She could keep the baby. She could keep the pregnancy and adopt the baby to another family. She could end the pregnancy. She didn't want to terminate her pregnancy, but she couldn't see any way out. She still had school to finish, an uncertain future in front of her, no job, an already fractured family. How would she tell her parents? Would her boy-friend still care for her? How would he feel about the baby? She didn't think he was ready to be a dad, and she knew she wasn't ready to be a mom. But how could she walk through the entire pregnancy and give this baby up?

An abortion seemed the only way to "take care of" this situation. In her mind's eye, this option provided the freedom for her to keep her circumstances thoroughly undisclosed and, after a brief recovery, to resume her life as normal. But she thought about her two friends who had aborted their babies, and the emotional scars they hid behind a lot of bravado and a kind of forced satisfaction with themselves. Tina felt very alone.

I asked her if she would like to see the baby on ultra-sound, and she said she would, for sure. As she reclined, her face conveyed how surreal this moment was for her as she stared at the screen, unprepared for what she was about to discover. After a few seconds of hazy, whitish blur, there appeared a small image. Tina watched in amazement as her tiny baby moved, not much bigger than a lima bean, little arm and leg buds clearly visible, fluttering heartbeat about 180 beats per minute, occasionally "bouncing" off the hammock inside the uterus. No words can describe the wonderment, the stunning surprise at seeing this little one, so perfectly formed, so tiny, so real.

Tina began cry, tears welling up and tumbling out, with all the pent-up emotion of the last two months. I took some pictures for her to keep. Whatever she chose, it would be a life-altering event, and such choices needed ample space. She was very interested in the written information together with clear pictures of babies at every stage of development, with detailed descriptions. I gave her numbers and names for counselors, social workers, financial assistance, churches, adoption agencies, and pregnancy aid groups. I told her I loved her and would help her as I could. As I watched her drive away, pictures in her hand, I prayed she would allow God to help her sift through her fears and uncertainties and to strengthen her during these next difficult days.

Tina returned several weeks later with a determination to maintain the pregnancy and to be open to choices at the end. She had carefully considered our conversation and understood that as she agreed to give this baby life, this baby would save her life. Already she was making more mature decisions about her schooling, her activities, her friends, her future. She put some things on hold, as this pregnancy would consume most of the next seven months. For now, she would devote her energies and her time to making the best choices and providing the optimum environment for her baby to grow inside.

Tina had gathered her wits and her courage and told her parents about the pregnancy. In their own dismay and pending divorce, they were not able to give Tina the consistent attention and support that would have been best, but she felt better for having braved the storm and taken responsibility, not only for these kinds of difficult conversations, but for whatever was coming down the road. She embraced the next months with commitment and passion. Several of her closest friends stood by her and continued to be there for conversation, fun, laughter, and tears. There were a few shopping sprees at the second-hand baby stores. Friday nights were occasionally reserved for pizza, their traditional hangout. Because she was expected to deliver in the summer, Tina was able to complete her junior year in high school and prepare for her senior year.

In the end, she agreed that adoption was the best choice for her baby, though very difficult. Both Tina and Gene understood that neither of them was prepared to be a great parent, and they both wanted great parents for their baby. They were both involved in this open adoption and felt confident that the couple they carefully selected would give their baby a stable and happy home.

A very warm and sunny July afternoon saw the beginnings of labor for Tina. She walked in the park around the wading pool with children splashing in the water and their mothers sitting nearby, ever watchful. She paused beneath the trees under the cooling shade of their large maple leaves. She marched up the gravel walkways between the fragrant rose bushes, stopping to catch her breath and smell the sweet yellow lace-wings and the heady tangerine Tropicanas. She sauntered down the path that gently sloped away from the soccer fields toward the grassy knoll by the large elm tree. She rested for a time while her contractions built up stream for the race down the track.

Soon, Tina was at the birth center, panting lightly through the tough ones, sighing deeply at the end. Her family walked alongside, her boyfriend holding her hand, her mother occasionally wiping her brow with a cool cloth. Her two close friends offered snippets of advice, and they smiled at some silly comment or two.

The couple Tina and Gene chose to be parents for this baby were present also, thrilled to be invited, excited at the life-changing event in process, barely able to contain their delight and gratitude. And when Hannah Rose, all seven pounds and thirteen ounces of her, finally made her grand entrance, there was an eruption of joy. Every moment was captured on film—the cutting of the umbilical cord by the new dad, Peter; the stamping of Hannah's long feet on a birth certificate; her first lusty cries and her soft suckling.

Tina had decided to give Hannah Rose the benefit of her colostrum and to take that time to say her gentle and tearful goodbyes.

Barbara, her new mom, held Tina's hand and hugged her. She stroked the baby's sleek black hair and kissed her soft cheeks. Tina and Gene would be able to enter adulthood knowing their baby would be safe in the arms of two extraordinary people who would lavish her with love and opportunity. Those three days seemed interminable, but they were an important closure moment for Tina and an opportunity for faith for Barbara and Peter.

This was certainly a bittersweet moment. Tina and Gene eventually went separate ways. Years later, Tina wrote me from Vermont, telling me that she had completed her schooling as a radiology technician and had an excellent job in the ultrasound department of a hospital nearby. She had found a special man to marry, and they were expecting their first child.

She maintained annual contract with Peter and Barbara at Christmas time, and Hannah Rose was doing wonderfully, now seven years old. Tina knew she had made the right decision, and she wanted to tell me what a blessing it was that day when she got a little peek at her baby on my ultrasound. She continued to keep her eyes open, she said, for the opportunity to bless others with her life and her work.

Blessed at Age 50

When I arrived at her home for a prenatal visit, Ferrin was hanging wash out on the line in the backyard. The spring breeze made the sheets flap wildly, the corners help tightly by old-fashioned clothes line clips, like the kind my grandmother used to use. Everywhere I looked, the beauty of simplicity surrounded this small enclosure. The narrow yard rushed down to the edge of the back bay on Pt. Orchard sound. Crocuses and daffodils popped their fragile heads out of the dirt, each carefully planted clump surrounded by small white rocks of different sizes and shapes. The larger borders were marked by round rocks painted pastel colors of blue and green and yellow and pink. Here and there clay garden statues of deer and rabbits and one small dog, probably a terrier, kept company with the vegetables soon to emerge from the well tilled soil. I sat on a half sawn cedar log, a bench Gavin had made many years ago. Now after all these sittings, the edges were smooth and inviting for an afternoon's visit. It was a lovely scene, and Ferrin soon sat down with me, welcoming the momentary respite from "the woman's work never done." This was her seventh pregnancy. She and Gavin had started their family a little late in life, when Ferrin was 38 years old, after completing lengthy educational goals. Gavin had a PhD in environmental management, and Ferrin's masters involved the education of children with special needs. In between babies, Ferrin was frequently called as a consultant by the schools and families in her small community.

I had met Gavin many summer ago when we were considering building a small cabin for my father in his old age. We had a large pond that lay between our house and this site for the cabin, and we wanted Gavin's expertise to design it properly. Many woodland creatures inhabited the 3 acres we enjoyed. Ducks loved our pond. And nearly every day, a large blue heron would come to stand on the edge of the pond, watching with consummate patience for the occasional perch to come close enough for lightning stab, and lunch. Our dog Boris would bark happily, from the safety of our side of the pond, and the heron would lift its huge wings, climb up into the sky and fly away over the cotton woods and fir trees. One summer morning we had beaver invade the privacy and quite of our pond, splashing furiously and gobbling up the fish we had so carefully put there the summer before. We only saw him once, that bright Saturday morning, while we watched from the deck overlooking the back yard, but we were just amazed. And one time we saw an eagle dive and catch one of our little wood ducks; its rainbow colors flashed in the sun as the eagle carried him aloft. Crickets and frogs sang at the top of their voices at night, to quiet suddenly when a fish jumped, or a cat slunk by.

Gavin assured us we could build this small space for my dad, and protect the myriad small life forms that brought us all so much delight. We talked a lot about life, the beauty of every form, the complexity, the simplicity, the perfection. And of course the conversation moved to the most magnificent of life, a small baby. Ferrin had come with Gavin on this visit, and she told me about her first two births in Kansas. She was clearly a strong minded woman, of great common sense and deeply held opinions honed by experience. Ferrin fought for her unmedicated birth the first two times in a small hospital in Lexington, Kansas. She wanted to deliver this third baby at home, and we agreed to match our skills: she would show me her canning and weaving and planting; and I would help her with her birthing. We learned a lot from each other over the years.

Ferrin and Gavin rejoiced over six boys in 9 years, four of them so far into my hands. They had moved from the Kansas prairie to Washington after completing their degrees, and together they hand-built a simple two-story house on a small narrow lot in Pt. Otchard, whose lawn "ran down to the sea." The upper floor was entirely encased in carpet: floor, walls, ceiling. It contained not a stick of furniture. There was a small door at each corner of this 25' x 25' room, which opened into a cubbyhole space, just enough room for a single bed, a bar for a few shirts, and a desk with small lamp. These were Spartan digs, to be sure. But the sense of it became apparent when the rains came, so common from fall through spring in the Pacific Northwest. This space made a racquetball court, a basketball court, a tennis court, a ping pong court, a wrestling mat, a boxing ring, an enclosure for crafts, a building site for small wooden toys (for one boy) a place to carve a violin (for another boy), or to design a 4-drawer cabinet (for yet another), a theatre for drama productions, a space for sleep overs with friends, all the while the noise of 6 boys muffled ever so slightly above the reading and music room downstairs.

Each of these boys, when they turned 9, began to train a seeing-eye dog for the blind. Then when the year-long training was complete, they made the trip with their beloved dog, and their parents, to California, to give the dog as a gift to someone who was blind and needed this dog for their safety, comfort, love and support. There were tears of parting, and tears of giving, and tears of receiving. I met these dogs in sequence, a yellow lab, a German shepherd, another yellow lab, a golden retriever. The dogs accompanied the boys at all times. The rule was: wherever the boy goes, the dog goes, including to bed—one more sensible reason for this great room.

Downstairs the enclosure held a kitchen and living room, pretty much all one space. The corner for reading, with shelves packed to the ceiling with books and magazines and reading material of every kind, daily for one hour hosted the music session with recorder, fiddle, cornet, and harmonica. There was a lot of music in this house, together with just plain noise. And now there was going to be another addition to the noise, the lovely strains of a baby crying.

Ferrin, at age 50, was pregnant with her 7th child, and all the boys were terribly excited about "who" was to come. But they all had agreed that this pleasant surprise needed to be just that. And although ultrasound was increasingly popular for identifying gender, Gavin and Ferrin and the boys had agreed Not To Know. Throughout the summer of this pregnancy, Ferrin canned peaches and tomatoes and beans and beets and pickles and just about anything that could fit in a jar. She put up salmon and halibut and herring. She dried apricots and bananas. She made pies with cherries and ate the rest. A few strawberries made it to the freezer, though these favorite fruits "always seem to be best when fresh," she said. Blueberries were canned and frozen, and made into cobblers for desert. The garden yielded lettuce and lettuce and more lettuce, so fresh and sweet. The radishes were pungent and hot, and the onions with their vibrant green tops were the garnish for every salad. Meanwhile the boys grew and grew, fished down on the Sound when they could, pushing out the small row boat that hugged the side of the garage in the winter. They milked Nanny, the Nubian goat that kept the blackberries mowed to a fine edge. And they waited. And they waited.

Ferrin didn't seem overly anxious to give up this Little Bean, now grown to a Big Squash. Normally a vegetarian, she was a tall woman, about 5 feet 8 inches, weighing about 125 lbs dripping wet. She kept herself healthy with a vigorous walk up the hill twice a week from their house to the main road and on down to the farmers' market about 3 miles away. There she bought what herbs she didn't grow on her windowsill, (parsley, wintergreen, basil, rosemary, and whatever special items her neighbors brought to market), along with potatoes, leeks, turnips, Hubbard and acorn squash, whatever didn't fit in her own garden. September 15th came and went, the full moon of that cycle briefly lighting the yard and shimmering on the water of the sound. Ferrin had gained more weight in this pregnancy than in any other, and she felt the strain of her growing belly, on her still skinny legs. She laughed when she looked in the mirror, she felt like a giant pumpkin on stilts. She had had a perfectly normal pregnancy in every respect, so she wondered if it was just her age that made her short of breath, and so bone tired in the evening. She loved feeling the baby kick, but felt a bit like a punching bag at times. Did this baby ever plan to come out?

After dinner and a slice of delicious apple pie that last Thursday evening in September, with the smell of fall hanging fragrantly in the air, Ferrin walked down to the dock. She loved watching the stars peeking out from behind the clouds that drifted on the wind. The sound of her neighbor's boat tapping at the dock in the dark made a rhythmic bump over the water. She listened to the distant bark of a dog, answered by a more distant coyote, like a song's refrain, calling, calling—but no baby. She didn't want October to come without a baby in arms, and she prayed.

Finally Ferrin gathered her skirt tightly around her, feeling the movement of this baby high in her ribs, and walked slowly up the yard, past the now finished garden, past the clay statues of deer and rabbit, up the steps to her kitchen. She could smell the remains of beets cooking on the stove, her favorite desert these days, as it had been with each of her pregnancies. She wondered at the tightening she felt as she sat down in her favorite green plush chair in the reading room. She wanted to refresh her remembrance of the story of Hannah. If this were a baby girl, she had selected Hannah as her name, loving the story of promise and gift with her baby Samuel, and God's sweet blessings to her in her anguish.

Gavin came to join her, and together they talked of the days' events, and the hope of the baby's coming soon. Ferrin remarked to Gavin that she could feel the baby move from time to time, in between some slight cramping. Her face was flushed and her voice had a slight tremolo. Gavin, ever her protector, recognized before she did that this evening would bring a Little One with it. They watched and waited for a while, reading favorite passages to each other over about an hour. Ferrin got up to get a final "bite of beet," and said quietly to Gavin, "It's time." They called me, and quickly I gathered my things and was on my way. Baby NO. 7 would not delay long, I was sure.

When I arrived within the hour, Ferrin was silent, pacing quietly the length of the kitchen-reading room, glancing periodically at the verse she had opened to, "Sorrow comes upon a woman in travail, but there is joy in the morning." The boys had gone down to their cousin's house, to await the Great News. There was a fire in the wood cook stove, little sparks visible under the tilt of the cast iron lid. Gavin had stacked wood for a month, it seemed, and the smell of cedar and fir, and the crackle of the logs brought a sense of comfort to the warm room. Ferrin wore a light green shift of cotton, which clung to the sweat on her shoulders. She paced, sipped warm chamomile tea with honey, leaned over the middle railing of the china hutch with contractions, and moaned ever so slightly with each exhalation. I took her vitals, her blood pressure normal, her baby's heart tones banging away at 150, and watched her slip into the dance created for this birth.

After about 45 minutes, Ferrin asked me to check her dilation, though she assured me she did not want to lie down long. Standing gave her the most comfort, and enabled her to continue her "dance" with purpose. Within seconds, I found that she was 8 centimeters, and I could tell her that soon she would have this baby. She sighed a great sigh of relief, and said, "I could have told you so." Her smile belied her tone, and the twinkle in her eye showed her gratitude. Ferrin paced some more, and then began to stand in place, reaching up to hang on the top edge of the hutch, and arch her back slightly with contractions. The guttural sounds she made at the back of her throat when each contraction reached its peak told us all that this baby was ready to come.

Ferrin decided that she wanted to stand for this birth, and so Gavin and I got ready a place for her, a platform of sorts, with towels, absorbent pads, receiving blankets warming on the top of the stove, and assorted birthing tools and equipment at hand. And we waited. Soon Ferrin began to heave with effort with each contraction, to apply that urgent pressure to her birth canal, and we could see the top of her baby's head when she pushed. This baby would be born with black hair, like all the brothers. They had swiftly turned to blond, the Norwegian heritage taking over completely by the time they were 2 months old. But for now, the black hair signaled the emergence of a beauty so serene and perfect, we all held our breaths, and pushed with her.

Gavin had his hands "at the ready," and Ferrin gave a powerful push. The baby's head emerged, but not quite. Hmmm. She pushed again, but the baby came no further. And again, just to the chin. Hmmm. I asked Ferrin to get onto her hands and knees. This was the Gaskin maneuver for stuck babies, named for midwife Ina May Gaskin, which is very successful in such difficult and emergent situations. Shoulder dystocia is no friend to moms or midwives, and with time of the essence, this baby needed out now. With great and magnificent effort, accompanied by strong encouragement from Garvin, Ferrin pushed three times more, and I could get the baby's posterior shoulder out, tight like sticky tape, with the cord wrapped twice. This baby did not fall out, as we had all expected. Instead, all 23 inches of this eleven pound baby got pushed out with heroic effort and the help of God. Ferrin and Gavin were thrilled with this 7th boy, who would fit so well into their family, and who appeared to be 6 months old already! They thought about Samson, but settled on Samuel, and felt entirely "gifted" with this baby.

Not long after, I visited Ferrin and Gavin and Little Samuel, to find him nursing like a pro, with a strong latch and excellent suck, like he knew exactly what was expected of him. His cute body just about covered the entirely of Ferrin's lap. The rainy season had begun and I could hear the boys upstairs bouncing a basketball against the walls and through the hoop at the end of the room, their vibrant boy voices calling back and forth to each other with that happy family tug-and-tease I'd come to recognize with my own herd of 4 boys.

This was the last of Ferrin and Gavin's babies, and the whole experience seemed completely fitting. Some years later I delivered a few of their grandbabies, and felt so blessed to have been a part of their lives. Whenever I drive by their house by the bay, though now it's gone to others, I remember that late September evening and revel in the birth of the Big Bean, The Gift at 50.

True Heroes

Birthing babies is women's business, is the old wives' tale. We've all seen the movie images from days gone by of the soon-to-be father pacing back and forth in the waiting room, sweat on his brow from worry, chain-smoking unfiltered Camels, and anxiously awaiting word from the doctor about his wife and his new son or daughter.

"It's a boy!" declares the man in the white coat as he briefly flashes an appearance before exiting again into the operating room. Knowing he cannot yet see his wife and baby, as they are being taken care of by the hospital staff, the proud new father begins to shove cigars into the hands of everyone he sees, chanting with joy, "It's a boy! It's a boy!" He quickly makes his way to the maternity ward, stopping only momentarily to pick up the largest bouquet of fresh flowers the gift shop has to offer.

Times have changed, and the culture now welcomes men into the realm of birth—not just as an observer, but also as an active participant whose contribution is huge and hugely respected. Even the most independent woman feels fragile and vulnerable in the face of labor and birth; the comfort and support she feels by her husband's presence and his kind words are deeply appreciated and her respect long lasting. In a maternity ward, a birthing center, an operating room, or their own home, these men are to be honored, thanked, and exhorted for their strength and ability to fully give themselves to the process, to help bring into the world their new little baby.

A man is the guardian of the family. Imbedded in his DNA is a desire to conquer obstacles, to find solutions for problems, and to supply ample provision for his family. He wants to protect and provide. It's no small wonder that men from past generations excused themselves from the labor process. During those long hours, he could neither suspend her pain nor hurry her work.

But today, a man wisely has come to realize his woman needs nothing from him except the love his presence offers. That he devotes himself to escorting her through the process, no matter how long it might take, means the world to her. And although his biggest role may be to simply sit by her side, after all is done, she will tearfully look into his eyes and gratefully say, "I could never have done this without you here." Laying aside his need to be a fixer, he follows her lead.

When couples surrender themselves to each other, a deep and lasting bond occurs between them. He watches the steely will and stamina of his wife. She sees his eagerness to help her at this most fragile moment. Some men unwilling to leave their wife's side have gone hours without a bite of food. Others have massaged her hips and lower back with more strength and endurance than any seasoned masseuse. My admiration for dads grows each time I watch them in a birth.

Occasionally, the job requires a bit of special effort and work. Several years ago, a couple came to my office; he at six feet four inches, and she at five feet five inches; they made an interesting "set of bookends." As a former college football player, he probably outweighed his petite wife by one hundred fifty pounds. While it's a tight fit the first time, usually babies manage to get born, aided by the heroic efforts of mom and everyone supporting her. God just made it that way. Maybe the baby will be six pounds, maybe ten pounds, and anything in between. But most of the time the baby just fits the pelvis he grows in. Occasionally moms can't get their babies out, and a cesarean section is necessary. The rate used to be about 4 percent; today the cesarean section rate is hovering above 32 percent and rising. Perhaps if moms had the opportunity for unimpeded hard work, as I've seen some do, they might be better able to complete the work without surgery.

Granted, some moms have to work harder than others. Liz understood that with this first baby, she might have a piece of work in front of her. Nevertheless, she expressly wanted a non-medicated labor. She did not want anything to impede her ability to "get the job done." I knew she could be successful, because she had the stamina of a trained athlete herself and the resolve to do work. As a marathon runner, she knew what endurance meant, she had "hit the wall" before and understood what it takes to get past that, and she was positive and strong, fully convinced that she could manage this labor and birth.

Liz had a healthy pregnancy. All her labs were within normal limits. She was never anemic, an otherwise common condition, and her glucose measurements were always boringly normal. She ate well and exercised regularly, taking frequent walks in her peaceful neighborhood under the shadow of Mount Rainier. Then, at forty weeks plus five days, her labor began very early in the morning, on a lovely Northwest summer day.

It was a perfect atmosphere to welcome a new little life with temperatures in the upper seventies, little humidity, and a soft breeze wafting through the windows. As her labor progressed, Liz took some contractions leaning against one of the pillars in her dining room. During the breaks between contractions, she munched on fresh strawberries and watermelon. Occasionally, she squatted near the ficus plant and plucked the wilted leaves as she counted in her head to that magic number when the pain would subside and begin to slide down the hill. Mostly, she walked in an ever-smaller circle around her kitchen, resting her elbows on the counter and looking past unseeing eyes to the fields behind her house.

By early afternoon, I knew she was nearly ready to bring forth their first son. Small beads of sweat appeared on her upper lip, and she became especially quiet and withdrawn as her contractions increased and her focus drew her inward. Those guests she had invited to her birth were still as stones, watching with amazement as she moved with the music of labor. She had asked them to be quiet when the contractions got intense. No one made a peep. Her husband followed her about, always at a respectful distance but ever ready with a strong arm to lean on, a neck to hang from, a soft word of encouragement, and a note of hope.

Soon Liz readied for the Herculean effort she anticipated to birth her big baby. Careful and frequent monitoring of both mom and baby continually assured excellent heart tones. As Liz moved into the pushing phase, her attitude remained positive and confident. She remarked that with each completed contraction, it was one down and one less to go. After nearly seven hours of labor, Liz began to feel the urge to push. She felt a surge of energy, a wave of power to help her finish the final business, and she was excited to be so close. And so began "The Work."

Liz pushed with all her heart and soul, with every fiber in her body, in every position she could manage; and each time there was a micrometer of descent that signaled "progress." She pushed on her side. She pushed semi-sitting. She pushed standing. She pushed squatting. She pushed on her hands and knees. She pushed lying on her back with her knees drawn up. I remember thinking, this woman is so determined to birth this baby; she would push while standing on her head if that helped!

With each contraction, her baby's heart continued its vibrant, steady beat with lovely normal variability. How reassuring that sound can be! Liz knew this pumpkin pie would be strong, and she wanted to be strong for him as well. With each push, Liz worked her baby down ever-so-slightly as her pelvis stretched, and her baby's head was molding…everything was in order, but oh, what work it took! And the time continued to pass.

Finally, Liz's husband, Mark, suggested another position, and this one gave her just the angle and the direction of force she knew would work. It must have been his professional football background. This stance required Mark to squat and bear all the weight of his pregnant wife as he balanced, completely unsupported, with Liz on his lap, and her legs outside his. He maintained this posture for an hour as his wife worked with all her strength to get their beautiful son out into their arms. He did not utter one word, nor trembled even in the slightest. I was astonished! His leg muscles must have been burning, but he never complained.

Surely, this was a monumental task for Mark as well as Liz; but that's what it took, and together they birthed a healthy, robust, hollering, eleven-pound baby. What jubilation! Everyone cried; tears of joy, relief, praise, excitement. Mark's strength, both physically and emotionally, in support of Liz's remarkable effort, enabled Sean to be born in a safe and natural setting, with the support of grandmother, two aunties, and two cousins present. Both parents felt victorious, and surely they were.

Exactly one year later to the day, Liz and Mark birthed their second son, Phillip, also an eleven-pound baby. As is usually the case, this birth was considerably shorter and easier, a gift for having worked so successfully through the first one. Once again, LIZ delivered while sitting on Mark's lap, and he was just as stoic. Must be what works for her! These boys will no doubt be the spitting images of their father, and what a splendid heritage to have.

Recently, I was helping another couple, both teenagers, and again met an amazing young dad. Paula, seventeen, and her eighteen-year-old boyfriend, Ray, had that star-studded look of young love, and they were exceedingly excited about this very planned baby. I wanted to give them the best experience, because this baby could open up vistas of responsibility and maturity to bind them ever closer and make the difference in our culture of easy "outs." I felt that if they achieved a healthy and happy birth with their baby, they would understand that together they could accomplish anything important for their family's future.

Paula's labor began about 10:00 a.m., a day before her due date, with ruptured membranes of clear fluid, but there were no contractions. Later, she came in for monitoring, which showed a perfectly happy and contented baby, except still no contractions. She waited patiently for several hours, walking to the park nearby, visiting with her sister-in-law, Kathy, who was also pregnant and due in two weeks. They talked about their plans for their little cousins-to-be, how fun to raise this boy and girl together. They talked about what labor might be like, and since Kathy had already had a birth with me, she could reassure Paula that she could except lots of hard work but a healthy outcome. "Safe and happy, in that order," she reminded Paula, the guiding mission in my practice.

By early afternoon, contractions began, slowly at first, about twenty minutes apart, but gradually increasing until they were coming consistently about four minutes apart. By this time, Paula and Ray had returned to the birth center. All vital signs were normal, and Paula was excited the process had begun. Her sweet personality was so evident in her attitude and demeanor. She seldom complained, even when the contractions became intense and necessitated all her concentration and effort. Only an occasional "ooooh" escaped her lips when she felt the peak of the pinch. Ray was ever present with her, encouraging her with his eyes, his hands on her back whenever she needed some counter pressure, his gentle and private words in her ear when she grimaced with pain.

Second stage began, and it was time to start pushing. After trying a number of positions, Paula was able to get the most out of her effort with a semi-sitting position. In order to facilitate her best efforts, Ray stood behind Paula and reached out around her so he could take a strong hold of her feet. This provided a semblance of squatting for Paula, while enabling her to rest in between pushed. Ray's back must have felt the strain, but he never complained, and he was up for every contraction.

For three hours this couple labored together like this. Each contraction brought their newborn "closer to the light," and each time her heart thumped strong and clear. With intense effort by everyone involved, Paula finally delivered nine-pound, six-ounce Amelia, with a beautifully molded head covered with silky black hair. She was spectacular, and Paula and Ray just looked at her with adoring eyes; then they looked at each other with adoring eyes. Both felt completely empowered as they both had had the physical workout of a lifetime. They did it together, and now they were a family.

Several weeks later, Ray took on a second job, leaving work at the cardboard box plant each afternoon to bus dishes at a local restaurant. He was determined to keep his little family together and solvent. Paula nursed Amelia into the robust, smiling cherub she was surely meant to be. I have great hopes for this young couple and pray for their continued union of love and work.

Birthing babies is definitely not solely "women's business." Labor is designed to engage both mother and father; both selflessly surrendering themselves to its miraculous, rhythmic progression. And no matter what the process becomes, how difficult, how long, one thing is certain: when that man comes face-to-face with his newborn child, he is entirely overwhelmed. Unlike almost anything modeled in today's media or pop culture, a new dad becomes wholly transparent as he tearfully gazes into the beauty of this heavenly creature. Taking in a deep sigh of relief, all fear or worry of the unknown for the moment is completely dispelled by his baby's first breath. In many ways, he will ever be the same again. For a good many, younger men especially, this moment can be the catalyst that propels him to take charge as his family's provider. In time he may commit himself to become the best father he can possibly be. That heritage can affect his children through generations and leave a true and brave legacy that can't be broken.

Culture and circumstances sometimes get in the way and put a damper on the event. But whenever possible, I encourage couples to consider that the crucible of labor can strengthen the bond of their relationship. It is a worthy goal. A healthy and happy birth experience can do so much to promote good for this new family. It is worth all the effort as both parents can use this moment as a benchmark and a memorial of the strength of which they are made. "Huzzah's!" to those moms and dads who catch this vision and run in the race to win.

The Third's the Most Charming

When I first met Kate, she had already delivered five strong, energetic boys. She was a wonderful mother who had remarried a few years earlier and was now quite excited about the news that she and her husband were expecting their second child together. They were a very close family, with no division between "yours" and "mine" and "ours." They would regularly pile into their eight-passenger van to go camping together in the pristine mountains, lakes, and shorelines of the picturesque Puget Sound in Northwest Washington. Ball games were a tumble of boys, bats, balls, and mitts, with their two pet Jack Russells thrown in for good measure. This positive pregnancy test just added to the vision they shared of filling their large home to the brim with happy, productive, loving children.

Being a mother of four boys myself, I found myself looking forward to visits with Kate, as we spent the time talking about our brood of boys, wondering what a girl would be like but not wanting to trade a one of these frog-loving, tree-climbing, mud-spattered, loud, and messy boys for any pink princess. We laughed a lot and shared funny stories as we waited for the time she could know who this Little Bean might be.

At twenty weeks, Kate and Stephen found out they were having yet another boy. Where they thrilled! A girl would have been a delightful surprise; but a boy they knew would fit right in with the pattern and mold they already had, and their deepest desires for him focused not on his gender but on his health—five fingers and five toes.

Kate began labor just two days before her due date. When I received her call early that morning, I knew I needed to respond quickly, since this was baby number six, and these ones can scoot out like a leaf on a waterfall. I arrived to a household full of excited children, grandparents, and friends. Stephen was almost breathless with anticipation; Kate was laboring peacefully in the bedroom; and I was glad I had hurried. When I checked her, she was almost ready to begin pushing this beautiful boy out into the world.

Just under an hour later, Kate and Stephen's brand-new baby boy emerged into the world and gasped his first breath. He was a vigorous eight pound and eight ounce, with perfect satiny pink skin and eyes just like his daddy's, almond shaped and dark. Within a few months, the other five boys had been introduced to this new member of the family, and the celebration began. Cameras flashed as the swaddled baby was passed from brother to brother, each smothering him with hugs and kisses. I snuck in with a footprint kit between passes, just to get those big feet on record. They named him William, brave and true.

About two hours later, conversation began to diminish, family began to whisper good-byes, and only Grandma remained, sliding silently on soft slippers between the boys, putting one to bed, encouraging another to finish a book, this one to tidy up his room, that one to draw a picture for mama and the baby. We watched Little Will nurse, looking around at his new surroundings. He sucked the sweet colostrum from his mother's breast, taking in his mother's smell and the feel of her skin on his. It was in this quietness I noticed him making a few different-sounding breaths, grunting almost. I listened more closely to find that as he continued to breathe, he seemed to labor a little. This was new, and it needed attention as his bright, pink skin began to pale ever so slightly. So I quietly picked up the phone and called my good friend and pediatrician, who was also their family doctor.

Anything that is unique in a baby always deserves a conversation. When the doctor answered, I told him what I had observed in this otherwise healthy term baby, and he suggested we bring him in for an examination. Surely there was nothing to worry about, but, like me, he believed it is always better to err on the side of caution with a newborn.

We bundled the baby, secured the car seat, kissed the other boys, left them in the care of Grandma, and went off to see the pediatrician whose office was only a few blocks away. After carefully checking William from his little top knot of brown hair to his big toes, the pediatrician pronounced him most likely fine but for good measure recommended he stay overnight at the local hospital for observation. There the baby would have the needed professional care should anything be amiss, or if his breathing became more labored and difficult.

Some time after being admitted to the hospital, Little Will's breathing took on a decidedly ominous tone, with audible forced grunts every breath, pallor, and a rapidly deteriorating condition. He was immediately transferred to the region's neonatal intensive care facility, where he was placed on life support while the physicians and experts present tried to determine what had happened to William. How had this once alert and vigorous baby changed so dramatically into an extremely weak and struggling newborn?

Shock and anguish covered everyone, prayers were offered, and the anvils of faith began to strike the nails of doubt. Many tests were done on his little body, trying desperately to uncover the menace that had struck so suddenly, rendering him helpless. Almost two weeks passed in this frustrating wait for answers, while he was protected on life support and in medically induced coma. Everyone at the hospital was extremely solicitous to the parents, deeply concerned, hopeful that a reason would surface soon.

Eventually a biopsy taken from William's lungs provided the answer. William had a genetic condition called Surfactant B Deficiency. This particular protein is responsible for the lung's ability to move air in and out, to expand and contract, much like the oil that enables a piston to move up and down in an engine. Without this vital lubricant, William could not exchange air and had no chance for survival. The specialist explained that this disorder results from a defective gene from both parents inherited by the baby, and in this phenomenally rare instance, both Kate and Stephen had each passed on such a recessive gene to little William.

How difficult, for these parents who so sought and treasured life, who desired to give all of themselves to their children, to be faced with the decision to remove that life support from their newborn. But after much discussion and prayer, Kate and Stephen allowed the medical personnel to disengage William's life support apparatus. Kate held him first, her tears dropping like pearls on his cheeks. Stephen held him and helped each of his older brothers to touch him and express their sadness. Friends each took their turns with him, kissed his sweet face, nuzzled his soft downy hair, and smothered his restful body with love during the lingering time this little boy took to bid us all good-bye.

The dark cloud that enveloped this family gradually blew away, leaving a permanent scar, like a knife cut on the arm, to be touched often, rubbed, remembering the all-too-brief time with William, but keeping that love for him safely tucked away under the scar.

Katie and Stephen were again pregnant nearly a year later. This time at her twenty-week ultrasound, everyone was overjoyed to discover they were having a girl! They elected to have an amniocentesis to determine the baby's status, since it was possible that this baby, too, could have inherited the same condition as her brother William. The first amniocentesis would ascertain whether the baby had received the faulty gene from her mother, and if positive, the second and much more complicated test would reveal if she had also received it from her father. This deficiency is rare, and there were only two centers in the United States that performed the paternal portion of the test.

The results took two to three weeks to come back. What a long wait that was! The first result established that this baby girl had received the gene from her mother. Kate and Stephen now had to wait with deep anxiety to find out if she also had received one from her father. While they waited, took walks to the park, played with their boys, took a weekend camping trip to the heavily wooded and beautiful fierce Deception Pass. The boys played in the trees, got as muddy as they possibly could, cooked hot dogs over an open fire, braved a brief rain shower, and thoroughly enjoyed this momentary respite from the waiting.

Finally, after several weeks, the result came; sadly, the test was positive. This baby girl had the same lethal conditions as her older brother. Everyone was in mourning.

Nevertheless, Kate and Stephen prayerfully elected to maintain the pregnancy, even though every day would be filled with sorrow. They cherished life, and although they knew this little girl would only have a few hours to live, they wanted to meet her face-to-face, eyes open wide. They knew that even a short time with this treasure would be worth it. They spent their time helping their other children come to understand the circumstances they were facing and taught them how to find hope and celebration, in spite of grief.

The best medical care in a high risk center could offer no hope for this baby, so Katie and Stephen began to plan for the birth of their little girl in the quiet and serene atmosphere of their home in rural Puyallup. I felt privileged to care for them throughout the rest of the pregnancy. At her regular visits, we discussed every aspect of this coming event. It was important to Katie that she be allowed to plan some details for this baby's birth. She didn't know how long she would live, and she felt that every moment was precious. So Grandma crocheted pink blankets, friends brought little pink baby gowns, pink booties, pink hair ribbons, pink onesies, pink candles, pink lemonade—pink was definitely the theme! I was humbled by their simple courage and their calm as they determined to take each day as it came, grateful for each moment.

About a week before her due date, Katie woke to the sure rumblings of labor. We quickly assembled. Katie labored in a pink bathrobe over pink nightgown. She had pink ribbons in her hair and pink candles on the stand. The cradle was covered with pink blankets, crocheted afghans in various shades of pink piled in the corner, and little pink socks waiting for little pink feet. Within a few hours, this perfectly glorious little girl burst into the world. She was, naturally, pink all over, her bright eyes were wide open, and she squalled with a symphony of noise. What a sweet sound!

There was no one shushing her, everyone rejoicing in the cacophony of her beautiful music. All the boys gathered around to delight in their sister, holding her, loving on her, whispering in her ears, kissing the deep dimples in her cheeks. The aroma of life enveloped this new little being, like a massive bunch of roses, pink, of course. She nursed a little, and we made footprints for her birth certificate. Katie dressed her head-to-toe in pink, savoring every single moment with her precious daughter. Piles of pictures were taken, trying to capture every nuance of her expressions…what a beauty she was! And then she began to fade, softly, persistently, over the next thirteen hours. Smiles and laughter and tears were all woven together with kisses, until finally Mariah gave a long sigh, and she was gone.

The church was standing room only, spilling out the door and down the block. For a second time, this man and woman arose to express their gratitude for those few short hours they had with their daughter. They spoke to everyone about how wonderful each moment was and what a joy it was to nurture life. They voiced their trust in God and their belief that He had called them to be great parents. Katie and Stephen expressed their hope to see that destiny come to pass, and everyone gathered around them with love and support.

But when they shared the news of their next pregnancy, they did not receive the encouragement from those around them as they had with the previous pregnancies. Many thought it irresponsible for taking the chance of bringing a baby into the world only to witness death. But Katie and Stephen loved their children, and they loved life. They were willing to go through the extreme pain and grief that the death of a child can bring, for the privilege of conceiving a baby who would have an opportunity to live a long life. Some get one hundred years, and some get one hour; they understood that all of it is precious.

As they reached the twenty-week mark, they decided once again to have the complex set of amniocentesis testing to determine the condition of their unborn child. They were delighted to learn they were having a boy and began the process of testing. However, this time they faced opposition from the medical community as well. Since they had made it quite clear that they would not terminate a pregnancy under any conditions, the facility refused to perform the tests, They stated their argument to the time, effort, and cost of the tests if the parents chose to maintain a pregnancy when Surfactant B deficiency was diagnosed. Katie and Stephen were continually prompted to terminate this pregnancy.

But grace appears in many places, and a physician who had helped with the amniocentesis during Katie's pregnancy with Mariah agreed to sponsor this hugely expensive testing himself. Needless to say, Katie and Stephen were very grateful. Now all that was left was to wait patiently for the results. Weeks went by, each day seeming longer than the day before. The wait was like holding your breath, each morning waking up wondering what the report would show, every evening hoping for morning and good news. The first test results from Katie showed that this baby boy had inherited her defective gene once again. The fate of this baby boy now rested in the results of the next test. Even more intense than before, every day was sprinkled alternately with hope and dread as they awaited the second test results revealing whether their baby had his daddy's gene as well.

Finally the news came. The test indeed confirmed that this baby had inherited his father's defective gene. However, this time, inexplicably and miraculously, in the process of inheritance, the gene had mutated to a nonlethal form! There was no medical explanation for this event, but this baby would *not* struggle to breathe, and unlike his two elder siblings, he would not quietly fade. Instead, there was every expectation that his lusty cry and holler of affirmation would be just the beginning of a long and productive life. With shouts of joy and deep gratitude, Katie and Stephen bowed their heads.

There are no words to describe the elation they experienced from this truly awesome news. They walked through the rest of the pregnancy on air, simply glowing with expectancy. Her labor was excellent. When the day arrived and labor was in full swing, we knew it would be brief and to the point. Katie called to alert me, and I quickly gathered my things and was out the door in a flash. Arriving at Katie's within twenty minutes, though it seemed like an hour, I found her nearly ready for the big event. She had previously prepared her room—actually the whole house—with balloons, confetti, glitter tape, and more. She had carefully put aside the pink and had decorated the table and bed and bassinet with ribbons blue, banners of green, and flowers of the brightest gold. When David was born, he just howled and howled, hardly taking a breath in between. No one minded a bit, and David's birth was one long continuous prayer of praise.

I continue to be inspired by the courage, faith, and unconditional love these two parents displayed as they stood on their convictions. They responded to the pain of death, not with bitterness and depression, but with an unrelenting determination to bring forth life, God willing. Throughout the years, I have met up with them and their brood of boys, and I know they are thankful for the opportunity they were given for life. Some years later they went on to have that girl they knew was waiting for them, and with so many attentive older brothers, she is indeed the proverbial princess. Her birth was heaven-sent, a jewel of perfection. I have treasured memories of my several years' walk with this family, and like a delicious aroma, they come back to me in the night. When I awake, I thank God for the privilege of sharing life with such wonderful servants as Katie and Stephen.

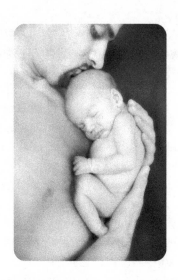

The Whispers of Knowing

What is the best care for this particular patient at this particular time?
This most important question continually circles in my mind. A
healthy pregnancy and birth require frequent assessment of every
woman's unique situation. The course of labor is a God-ordained,
miraculous design, which for the most part, takes care of itself. It needs
little intervention. A good midwife is an enthusiastic cheerleader,
offering support, information, love, and kindness, only occasionally
needing to provide medical assistance. Generally, my time during a
labor is spent offering encouragement, providing the mom with the
information she requires to be reassured everything is progressing
normally, and sharing suggestions which will help her move forward
toward birth in a timely manner. And then every once in a while,
a specific midwifery procedure becomes helpful in a challenging
situation.

　　Several years ago, I was given a gift from a friend who had
traveled extensively, mostly in African countries. I cherish this small

container, the size of a box for wooden matches. This cardboard receptacle, the midwife's birth kit, holds a clean piece of twine about ten inches long, a sharp razor blade, and a piece of plastic that unfolds to about three feet square. Expectant moms in many countries place their confidence in the midwives who carry little more than this kit but who bring a love for these women and babies that no container could hold. Good hygiene, cleanliness, education, and available medical care are great blessing, not shared by everyone. They indeed save lives and we could wish such medical technology were available to all the world. What a difference that would make! Still, the little box I treasure is a ready reminder that this natural process seldom requires much intervention and that love and attention are as much a gift to birth as medical technology.

Although the process of labor is a perfectly orchestrated natural event, every single one possesses its own rhythm, its own song. I have cared for some moms through quite a few births, being twice blessed to help two moms through each of their twelve labors. Yet every birth experience is unique. I always ask: What is the best care for this particular patient at this particular time? Sometimes there's a "gut feeling," sometimes an "intuition." That still, small voice that guides me into better decisions seems sharpened over time and many births. I pray every day for wisdom.

When Joanna and Will came in for their first appointment, I could tell from the look upon his face that this was Will's first child. Although he was about sixty years old, he had never experienced fatherhood. His recent marriage to Joanna, a little more than twenty-five years his junior, offered this life-changing event. While Joanna had two other children, now in their early teens, this was the first pregnancy for Will and Joanna together. Though it was certainly a surprise, they were ecstatic. Will diligently asked every question he could think of about the natural birthing process, along with anything else pertaining to Joanna's welfare. He was determined to be involved in every conversation.

During Joanna's pregnancy, she had an ultrasound at twenty weeks, which revealed a normally growing baby girl. Her older brothers were thrilled. In addition, the ultrasound revealed a small ovarian cyst. I sent Joanna to my obstetrician for evaluation of this cyst, and he determined that it should be watched but no management was necessary at this time. He agreed to keep an eye on her, and periodic ultrasounds indicated that this cyst was not growing.

Her pregnancy progressed normally, and soon she was term, due to have her baby. We had been having discussions throughout her pregnancy about Joanna and Will's desires for the day of delivery. As the time drew near, I had another conversation about it again with my obstetrician. Though there appeared no particular medical necessity, we all four agreed that a cesarean section might be in Joanna's best interests. While the cyst had not grown in the pregnancy, it was a small precaution to deliver by cesarean section, and both Joanna and Will accepted this recommendation.

Because this plan was made prior to the start of labor, the surgery proceeded with a sense of calm. The anesthesiologist held Joanna's head up so she could see her little girl newly delivered. Joanna was able to hold her soon after. I took pictures of Mom and Baby by the score. After Bella was delivered, the surgeon removed the cyst on Joanna's ovary. It was completely self-contained, only attached merely by the narrowest thread. It appeared quite benign. The tissue was sent to pathology for routine evaluation.

Within a few days following the cesarean birth, Will and Joanna received the results from the laboratory tests performed on the cyst. It revealed an aggressive cancerous tumor. This was a surprising diagnosis, yet ovarian cancer is often a silently striking phantom. Usually by the time it's recognized, the cancer is beyond repair. Joanna had a full hysterectomy eight weeks later and a complete recovery.

Today, Will and Joanna continue enjoying the benefits of life and good health. Bella is now in her twenties, going off to college and her future. For some time following Bella's birth, Joanna and I would connect, always marveling at the little intuition, born of grace and experience that gave her space. It's so nice for me to be at the bottom of the heap, to be able to seek the advice and expertise of the wonderful physicians I work with, and to be able to come up with the very best plan for every one of my moms.

The importance of conducting midwifery practice alongside the excellence of other medical experts cannot be overstated. One of the saving graces for a midwife is the mandatory requirement to consult with a physician whenever any situation deviates from "normal" in either mother or baby. This safety net enables the wisest decisions to be made in a team setting. Such a supporting network of physicians, pediatricians, hospitals, midwives, childbirth educators, lactating specialists, doulas, and others deeply involved in the care of mothers and their newborns provides a screen for detecting problems, a venue for solutions, and a framework for action when necessary. Each person in this wide group of "specialists" has a particular point of view, a depth of education and experience, and a desire to bring the best of what they have to the baby business at hand. It's encouraging to be able to call, on a moment's notice, any of these professionals for advice, counsel, constructive criticism, peer review, and wisdom. "Safe and happy"—safety first, happy when possible: that's the goal.

On a wintry day several years ago, a storm came blowing out of the Cascades, sheets of rain striking at angles against the windows, water running in rivers down every surface. Margie and Robert arrived at the birth center, bags in hand, in active labor. This was their third baby and it was a girl. Her soon—to—be older brothers that were now at Grandma's were excited to see her soon. Pregnancy is so long for those three—and four—year—olds, but finally the big day had arrived. Rebecca was born with luscious pink skin, robust responses, and alertness with wide—open eyes looking around at everyone. She was born at term, just three days past her expected birth date, and the labor was straightforward with no complications. The newborn examination was normal in every respect, except for one item: this little girl didn't seem to have a sucking reflex. Try as I might, I could not get her to suck, even on my finger. She just would not nurse; instead, she lay contentedly at her mother's breast looking up at her with bright eyes.

I could not let her go home with her family until she was nursing well. Some babies know instantly how to latch on and suck, some others take a little time to learn. We worked on this for several hours, and Rebecca just wouldn't, or couldn't, nurse. So I contacted her pediatrician. After some discussion, the family agreed to have Rebecca transferred to the special baby care unit of our local hospital. To everyone's bewilderment, Rebecca simply was unable to suck. This was not a case of "wouldn't" but "couldn't." Her swallow mechanism was out of sync, and she spent several weeks at the hospital, eventually being sent home with a feeding tube. A hospice arrangement with twenty-four-hour nursing care was begun.

What followed was also a surprise. Over the next few years, Rebecca had a number of episodes of breathing difficulties, infections, and hospitalizations, and eventually underwent jaw surgery. She had in-home care for about six years. A diagnosis was never made. Her condition never fit any known profile. She received great care at the hospital from various physicians and providers. But that first day, when she was sent to the hospital instead of to home, was lifesaving. With a few setbacks, and a scary event or two, she just got a little better every day after that.

Margie had two more babies with me, so her schedule was pretty busy. Rebecca continued to grow full of spit-fire and pizzazz. Even while needing care, she wrestled with the boys and stood her ground. She developed a fiercely independent spirit and was fully engaged in life.

Each year in August, the one hot month of summer in the Northwest, I hold my annual picnic. It is such fun to see babies "all grown up," sometimes now even adults, enjoying the day visiting with one another, playing in the grass, their mothers sharing stories and pictures. At one of these reunions for moms and babies when Rebecca was about five years old, her mother came running across the grass to me. Something remarkable had happened, she said in a trembling voice, "Rebecca swallowed on her own for the first time today at your picnic." What seems like such a simple action brought us to tears as the long years of challenges began to show future promise. That experience was extremely moving given everything this family had endured over the preceding five years. Such a window of beauty and love could not have been bought at any price.

The Bridge to the Finish

I cannot believe this is happening! I was on my way to deliver a baby in Gig Harbor, a small town on the Olympic Peninsula. To get there, I had to cross the Tacoma Narrows Bridge, once called "Galloping Gertie" because of its tendency to rock to and fro with the winds. In the 1940's, this bridge had swayed too far in the strong winds that whipped through the narrows and collapsed. The one photo of that event is eerie, like a Twilight Zone movie, showing the bridge deck all twisted and contorted, with parts of the supports hanging precariously and some of the bridge already collapsing into the white-capped waters of the Sound hundreds of feet below. The subsequent bridge, which I was now crossing, was a beautifully and safe crafted replacement, with plenty of give for the winds. The drive was lovely, looking at the Olympic Mountains visible over the trees when going west, and Mount Rainier standing majestically through the arches of the bridge when traveling east.

For so long, this bridge has been both a passageway to Gig Harbor and the peninsula towns beyond, and a restraint of sorts to too much traffic. The small hamlets beyond the quaint town of Gig Harbor are as inviting as they are hidden, and getting there is half the fun. Today there is a companion bridge, similar in form and shape, that makes the drive less crowded and access easier; but before the second bridge was completed, driving across the Narrows seemed to take forever, especially when in a hurry. Baby's coming!

On such a day, a decade ago, halfway across the bridge, traffic was completely stopped. Since the bridge was the only avenue to travel to the peninsula, once on it, there was no way out except to wait. Traffic had not moved for quite some time, and drivers were starting to get out of their cars to walk around...*never a good sign. I'm going to miss the birth,* I thought. *I'm actually going to miss the birth.* I sighed a deep sigh of disappointment as I began to resolve the situation within my heart and decided to join the folks on foot to find out why we were all stranded like this on the bridge.

There had been an accident a few miles ahead of the bridge on the far side, and it would be at least an hour before we started to move again. I called my patient's home and Dan, her husband, answered. From the information I gathered, I estimated the baby would come in the next hour. Heidi was completely at peace (this was her third baby, and she had delivered the previous two with me), and both were fairly confident all would be well until I arrived. We discussed calling 911, but as I could not get to them, neither could they get out to anywhere else, and Dan and Heidi elected to sit tight and wait.

If only this was a first labor, I'd have more time, I thought. But as Heidi's first two babies were quick births, I knew this one was going to come easily and rapidly as well. The good news about a quick labor, however, is that there are rarely complications. These babies, eager to sprint toward the entrance, are usually happy, robust newborns, perfectly pink and ready to shout their first cry, "Here I am!" One minute the water breaks, and the next they come out practically dressed and lying beside you. It's the long, drawn-out labors, after hours of hard work, when fatigue and dehydration set in, that are troublesome. But this was definitely not Heidi's scenario.

I stayed in contact with Dan and Heidi over the next many minutes. My hopes were elevated as traffic began to move; however, when I was about five minutes from their home, Dan let me know he needed to put down the phone because Heidi was sure she needed to begin pushing. And sure enough, I pulled into their driveway just as little Nathan took his first breath. I quickly unloaded any needed equipment and tended to all the post-labor necessities for this very thrilled couple. All were perfectly healthy and invigorated! The placenta was almost ready to exit as I walked in, and after several more minutes, came out easily.

Nathan was howling, and his raucous noise was like band music. He seemed destined to play the drums or the trumpet when he was grown. He was pink all over, even his hands and feet. His heart was thumping at a satisfying 150 beats per minute, his breathing a refreshing fifty-six breaths a minute. Very soon, Nathan was snuggled up next to his mom, happily nursing, quiet and content. Eye ointment and vitamin K were administered, and Nathan was warmly dressed in his father's first dressing gown. I am amazed, in this throw-away society, that such things are saved, but it is a treasure to watch the delight when special hand-me-downs are brought out for new ones. It seems part of the celebration, a personal moment that brings the family full circle. The little embroidery that great-grandma put around the neck and sleeves, some of it frayed a bit on the edges, just added a little extra love.

Along with that sweet first outfit, packaged like precious ointment, comes the gently given advice and wisdom of moms and grandmas, aunts, even uncles and grandpapas. In this event, I knew Heidi would be safe and well, since she was surrounded by her mom, Kathrine, and her grandma, Lucille. It was Lucille who had nurtured in Heidi her confidence and peace that birth is a normal natural event, which just comes along all on its own most of the time.

I relished the several conversations we all enjoyed over warm comfrey tea and gingersnaps as Lucille talked slowly and deliberately about her own births. She had had seven children and she quietly shared some of the poignant details of these experiences. Her longest labor, Lucille recalled, was her first one, when she paced the kitchen for what seemed like hours, while her husband paced in the garden, waiting for the midwife to come. It seemed to take from noon when the sun was high in the Kansas sky to midnight as the moon drifted between the clouds for her body to finally give up its sweet occupant. She learned patience from that birth.

Her second and third births were swift and powerful, like summer lightning. She recalled the drive to the birthing home in Madras, Illinois, where the nurse, an apprentice birth assistant, stood on the porch watching for her arrival. She ushered Lucille into the clean, quiet room, a cast iron bed with fresh sheets waiting for an occupant. Mavis was the local midwife, who seemed to have lived before time, draped in wisdom and kindness. She over-saw the preparation of the bed and the pans of hot water, the instruments for the delivery, and strips of pillow ticking for the baby's umbilical cord, with some to tie around his fat little belly to guard his navel. Her wizened hands folded the towels and blankets, getting everything ready for the new baby. Lucille was thankful for the fresh smelling sheets and the daisies in the canning jar on the cabinet. Mavis was full of humor and goodwill, such a blessing in birth. Lucille learned gentleness from these births, a boon in time to come with three wild boys.

At the birth of baby number four, Mavis laughed out loud, a big throaty laugh brought up from the depths of her ample lap, when she handed this little one to her mother. She used the corners of her big white apron, bleached clean in the sun for just this purpose, to wipe the little head and clean the nose and mouth. Then she placed this baby on her mother's breast and laughed again that full, deep laugh. Lucille's fourth baby was a girl, and after three noisy rambunctious boys, Lucille welcomed the opportunity for frills, pink ribbons, and the dream of tea parties to come. She learned thankfulness with this birth.

When she described her fifth birth to Heidi, she smiled broadly and reflected on the marvel that was this child. For this baby boy was her biggest by far, nearly eleven pounds, and he seemed to bounce into this world like a big red rubber ball. His first smile at barely two weeks lit up the sky. Everyone wanted to play with Lenny. He seemed to have pogo-sticks for legs, which Lucille was certain he had perfected while inside. She learned joy with this boy. She was glad her husband took up packing Lenny's sturdy frame to give Lucille's back a rest.

Grandma Lucille was quiet, contemplating something distant in her mind as she recalled her sixth baby, a tiny little one, too early, too small, too fragile. She laid her in a wicker basket with a yellow flowered receiving blanket. She'd tied blue ribbons to the selvedge. She cried and cried, mostly hot tears in the quiet of the night, while her husband laid his big hand on her hip and comforted her with tender words. She learned peace. All things are in God's hands.

Number seven was thoroughly unexpected, coming in Lucille's forties, reminding her to look out for the blessing racing around the corner; it's sure to whap you in the heart. This girl, feisty and fine, Heidi's mother, was hardly still a moment as a child, Lucille recalled. Lucille's enduring memory of that pregnancy was feeling like a couple of Clydesdales were running to the barn for dinner. Kathrine gave her mom and dad a spin for their money, full of life, a good bit of mischief, the usual ups and downs, with a dogged determination and stubborn will. Whew! Lucille learned persistence with this one.

Lucille was glad now that Heidi had inherited Kathrine's positive attitude and sharp intelligence. Lucille was especially close to her granddaughter Heidi, and she felt honored to be invited to the births of these great-grandbabies. Her advice and counsel spanned the generations with ease, and Heidi looked forward to afternoons with her grandmother. They could discuss most anything with candor and humor and a few chocolate chip cookies. Heidi loved to hear the stories her grandmother had saved up for her. Lucille wanted Heidi to look forward to her babies, to their births as well as their growing-up, and she felt a small urgency as the days and years passed.

My reverie was jolted as the traffic began to move. I knew the bridge was sturdy, and I knew Heidi and Dan were in perfect company; all would be well. So then, just missing Nathan's first breath, even by a few moments, felt rather like running a marathon side-by-side with a good friend, only to fail crossing the finish line together. But the confidence I had in this peaceful process was amply rewarded by the sight of four generations just loving on each other to beat the band. The affection that grows daily with these little cherubs softens that first bit of missing and makes each further breath all the more precious.

Before I left that evening, I got to wash little Nathan's full head of hair, to bathe his precious skin ever so gently, and to wrap him in a blanket that was his great-grand-mother's; bundled in this yellow flowered blanket with blue ribbons on the selvedge made Nathan look like a bunch of daisies. I could see the tears in Lucille's eyes, which she quietly wiped away with her kerchief. I hugged Heidi and her mom, Kathrine, thankful for the treasure of another sweet baby to bless the world. Heidi had worked hard, and her mom had been able to step aside enough to give her room. I kissed Lucille with a heart full of gratitude for what she had taught Heidi, for sharing the truth with her granddaughter, and for encouraging her to be the best she could be. The thread of wisdom got passed from one generation to another—straight, perfect, and fine.

The next evening, I sat with a young woman I'd known since her birth two decades earlier. I remembered the morning she was born and how like her mother's her long narrow fingers were, how graceful they looked in repose, even brand new. Now it was her turn, and I watched her wrap her lovely fingers around her husband's hand as she labored to have her own baby. This generational experience is especially intriguing to me as I observe the soon-to-be grandmothers struggling to maintain a distance and calm. It is difficult to watch her daughter work so hard, even though her daughter is now an adult having her own baby.

It seems just perfectly parental to want to absolve our children of pain, sorrow, hurt. We have to be careful we don't rob from them the thing they need most. Moms especially would step up in a heartbeat and take the pain, but there's really nothing to do but brave the passage of time and let it be. In due course, the process is finally complete, her daughter has become so much more a woman than ever before, all eyes are moist with pride, and everyone is thoroughly relived at the safe and perfect passage of this child into the world. The copious tears are also for another bridge that's been crossed, the transition to a new phase of womanhood.

Parents want their children to mature into caring, loving, responsible grownups. The process, which has value, is riddled with hazards of all sorts. So it is especially poignant to witness the change that takes place the instant the baby is born. Suddenly, like falling off a cliff, the new mom and dad become possessive, protective, proud, passionate, and private with their baby. It's everything right and good, deeply emotional, and totally blessed.

During the labor, the soon-to-be grandfather paces outside the room, wringing his hands, drinking way too much coffee, trying to distract himself with a magazine he's not really reading to pass some time. All the worry is rewarded, however, the moment this brand-new baby is presented by his parents to his grandparents. The sensation of deja-vu is striking; the cycle beginning and repeating in perfect harmony.

Since then, perhaps two dozen babies I had delivered have grown up and had their own babies with me. Each time, I marvel at the plan God has for His children. These little ones begin like a pencil dot, and they come out looking just like mom and dad—with the same dimples, the same expressions in their eyes, the same elongated toes, the same cowlicks, the same "angel kisses." Some babies have a birth mark that exactly resembles the parent's, in the same place. I remember the new parents as babies, often rummaging through some boxes and hauling out faded pictures taken of them some twenty or more years before. It's awesome that these new babies look just like their parents. It takes my breath away.

One day, a young couple came to the birth center for their first prenatal appointment. When I looked at the young man, he seemed so familiar, but because they had a common last name, I just could not place him. But I said, "I know you." I had delivered him twenty-four years earlier. He had the same facial expression, the same cleft in his chin, the same look in his eyes as when he was born, although now he had a mustache. He was just like shrink art in reverse.

For these generational births, two things have happened, of course: the moms conveyed positive birth stories to their children as they grew; and the families didn't move away. Now the children's turn has come, and they've chosen to birth in the same way. Whenever I cross the Narrows Bridge, I think of Heidi and Dan and remember Lucille with affection. I hope all grandmothers can pass to their daughters and then to their granddaughters the confidence in the cycle of life that ever flows around us.

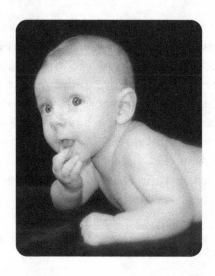

The Apple of Her Eye

For quite some time, I watched Ranee. She was about thirty-five years old, with medium brown hair combed in a soft pageboy style. There were just the beginnings of a few gray hairs at her temples. She sat among a group of ten women, all chatting easily at a summer luncheon about the business of women's work: raising children, loving babies, helping elder parents, teaching teenagers, engaging young adults, and other relationship issues that occupy the time and hearts of most mothers. Her face had such a calm about it, a reverence that almost made one look away.

Ranee added a few comments here and there, passed the tea cozy to her neighbor, taking a sugar cookie off the plate behind. Someone shared a sweet story about her two-year-old, and Ranee laughed with a story of her own. Her two girls were now teenagers, thirteen and fifteen, yet she remembered lovely details of certain events as if they happened yesterday. There must be a notebook of memories in the minds of mothers that collects the pictures and sweet minutiae of their children's experiences; just a thought or another's comment brings them out to be shared quickly and sweetly, like berries freshly picked.

I had come to know Ranee and her husband, Karl, over a several-year span and watched them raise their daughters to be interesting, challenging, beautiful, and active young ladies. They were very different from each other, as children are wont to be, taking some characteristics from great grand, some from auntie, some from papa, and some from mom. The marvelous and enigmatic blend of attributes that makes each one completely unique is best demonstrated among families, whose physical resemblances sometimes mask a wide variation of personality and temperament.

Such was the case with Ranee's daughters, Katie and Annie. Each had bright blue eyes and blond hair, one wavy, the other straight. Each was active in sports at school, volleyball being Katie's favorite, and soccer Annie's. The girls did well in school, consistently appearing on the Principal's List of Achieving Scholars. Katie preferred history, especially about America's founding, while Annie loved to write poems. Annie frequently left letters and small rhymes for her mother, to whom she was especially attached. At thirteen, Annie still had a child's heart, while beginning to grow into a young woman. At times she would dissolve into tears and then, within moments, she would be laughing heartily with friends. Katie retained the serious nature of her father and loved to debate. At fifteen, she thought she might like to be a lawyer, and her parents encouraged her to pursue her dream. Books and magazines littered her room, and she liked to take one side, and then the other, in conversations with her parents. Katie felt particularly protective of her mother and never failed to visit her mom before bedtime and kiss her goodnight.

Ranee and Karl felt thoroughly blessed with their daughters. Yet they realistically approached the challenges of bringing girls to adulthood with their hearts intact. Like all attentive parents, they spent most waking moments talking with, praying about, fussing over, and generally engaging their daughters in talks about life and the importance of right values and future obligations. There was always time for school events, the semester's drama production, a music performance, and their athletic contests. Their days seemed completely full, with "Occupied" hung visibly on the door of life.

So with great anticipation they sat down with their girls two months ago to discuss a decision of great impact they intended to make. Ranee and Karl wished to have another baby. Katie and Annie were intrigued but not surprised. Their mother had always been enamored with babies, any baby, and could barely restrain her delight when a friend announced a pregnancy or introduced a baby at church. Ranee's face lit up when she talked with her daughters, but she was completely frank and direct as she explained to them what impact this pregnancy would have on the girls. Already, they were very helpful in the home, but a new baby would take up considerable time and attention.

While she was extremely adept at navigating through life, adding a baby to the mix would certainly afford new excitement and new challenges, in particular because Ranee was blind. She kept her home quite clean and uncluttered so that she could maneuver the hallways and different rooms without bumping into anything unexpected. She knew what each cupboard contained, where each item was on the shelves, and where all the dishes were, placed in order of size and purpose. She had organized the closets so that with a touch she could recognize the sweaters, the coats, the shirts, and shoes each family member needed, and she had a keen sixth sense for anything that was out of place.

Ranee had not always been blind. As a child she had a weak left eye and wore thick-lensed glasses by the time she was in high school. After she married and had their first daughter, she went back to the local community college to finish her associate degree in sociology. One rainy day in early December, as she walked from one class to another, she tripped on a stone on the sidewalk and fell, ripping the retina of her left eye. There was no repair, and she learned to depend on her right eye entirely. Undaunted, she completed her degree just about the time she was ready to give birth to her second child.

After Annie was born, Ranee stayed at home and reveled in being a mom. One afternoon, she heard Annie crying in her crib, and as she came out of the hallway, she failed to see the door to the pantry closet open. She walked straight into the door, tearing the retina of her right eye. Several eye surgeons examined her, but they were unable to repair the damage. Ranee realized that she would be forever without sight; but with the loving and continuous help of Karl, Ranee managed to forge a routine that enabled her to care for herself, her husband, and her daughters.

Now more than a decade later, the girls were teenagers, and Ranee and Karl began to think seriously about having another baby. They knew without qualification this experience would not be easy, and there would be challenges most other parents did not face. But they felt confident they would be able to give another baby the love and attention they had been able to shower on their daughters. In addition, they had already learned through experience how to handle some of the difficulties that blindness entails. After much thought, consideration, conversation with their girls, and complete agreement by the entire family, they decided to proceed, God-willing.

Now at this luncheon, I watched the ease with which Ranee interacted with her friends. They treated her as completely sighted, talking with her about colors of dresses, furniture shopping, designs of clothing, matching outfits, planning weddings, arranging outings, making dinners, all the kinds of conversations common and free among friends.

I recalled the story told to me recently, in which Ranee's friend Bonnie was sitting at a red light waiting for the green, when a car turned left in front of her. She looked at the driver out of the corner of her eye and exclaimed to her husband, "Why, that's Ranee! I wonder where she's driving to?"

Only after a pause in the conversation—and a perplexed look from her husband—did Bonnie realize that it couldn't have been Ranee driving, just a look-a-like. But everyone who knew Ranee felt so completely confident in her ability to do whatever she put her mind to, the idea of her driving actually made sense for one brief second. I thought how this story was a testimony to the power of Ranee's composure and the strength of her will. So as I observed Ranee this summer afternoon and saw her love and grace, I realized that she would indeed be able to have another baby and raise that child with confidence and with the help of her husband and her daughters.

The following week we had our first prenatal visit. At each following meeting, Ranee grew more talkative and excited about the upcoming event, sharing the joy she felt about this baby. Ranee kept a journal of her thoughts, what kinds of things she wanted to achieve for this Little One, what plans she and Karl had for this baby, what dreams and expectations and hopes she harbored in her heart. When the time neared for the delivery, we set up the room, holding a "mock" birth, so that we (well, mostly me) would know where things were, what to expect, how the event might proceed, and what to do "if" something different or unexpected occurred. Ranee's other senses were especially heightened, and she could "feel" what was happening in the room and how everyone else was doing. When her labor began, her daughters got everything ready, Karl called me, and they put on some soft music to accompany the event.

As Ranee swayed to the rhythm of her labor, she hummed little phrases of love. When the birth pains accelerated, her voice became louder, as if to trumpet to the world that a new being was soon to be here. The anticipation grew, each contraction closer and stronger and longer, until they seemed to meld into one. Ranee's song rose to a shout as her baby tumbled into waiting hands and then was placed gently onto her heaving chest.

Everyone cried and laughed and hugged. This little boy was all fuzzy with little bits of birth "fur" on his ears, his shoulders, his forehead, and his nose looked a little crooked and his ear a little curled. He seemed to unfold a bit at a time, like a wild rose. I watched with awe as Ranee ran her fingers over his beautiful body, caressing his head, his face, his hips, his eyes, "seeing" his arms and hands and toes and knees and back and belly and chin and cheek; tasting the saltiness of his skin; delighting in the sweet smell of his hair. She pulled him to her breast and, as if he had always known how, he latched and began to nurse. She covered him with a soft sky blue blanket she had crocheted and continued to croon her little love phrases in his ear. Karl wiped his tears with the back of his hands as he fluffed her pillows and covered them both with a warm down quilt. He brought her warm lavender tea and toast with manuka honey from New Zealand. He adjusted the music, bowed his head with thanksgiving, and announced that his son's name was Ethan, strong and steadfast.

And that was how Ethan grew, firm and confident. His mother encouraged him as all mothers do, and he developed into a strong and steadfast young man his parents had prayed him to be. He learned his father's patience and kindness as he got older, and kept his mother's good humor and strong will. He had a mischievous streak, with no meanness in it, and his sisters were continually watching out for him. He was six when his sister Annie left for college to study nursing and eight when Katie passed the bar exam. The family moved to Colorado when Ethan was almost ten, and I hear he was remained, as always, the apple of his mother's eye.

Hurry Up and Wait

The ultrasound results were surprising. Not alarming, but certainly a bit unusual. At twenty weeks, Joelle's second pregnancy was progressing normally, and she expected to have as uncomplicated and wonderfully undramatic a course as she had with her adorable little boy, Evan, now twenty-three months. He was a spit-fire! The typical little boy just on the verge of spilling out the dozens of words he'd accumulated, a cascade of sounds as he chattered from dawn to dusk. His vibrant energy filled the household from the moment his big brown eyes opened under his thick black lashes to greet the day. Peeking out from around his mother's swelling belly as she bent down to kiss his curly brown hair, he tiptoed on the edge of their daily game of "Chase the Rabbit" before snuggling in her generous lap for a story before naptime.

But this day, Joelle skipped the chase, putting Evan to nap with his favorite story friends, *Frog and Toad Together*. She and her husband, Bryan, were scheduled for a conversation with their midwife about her recent ultrasound, and she wanted to have undivided attention to hear what the report identified. The radiologist had shown them a perfect baby, carefully and discreetly hiding the gender as these parents wanted the "surprise" still in the package four and a half months from now.

This new person had ten toes that they affectionately called "Popsicle Toes" after the popular song. With ten fingers, a beautiful spine, lovely brain structures, a four-chambered heart with the values flapping perfectly, this Little Being was nestled in a safe environment of salty water just right for growth and development. The placenta, their baby's ideal grocery bag, was secured to the front surface of her uterus, neatly out of the way of trouble and providing exactly what the baby ordered for a direct lifeline to health. However, clearly evident on the scans as well, was a cone-shaped cervix, 40 percent effaced and one centimeter dilated. This was a surprising discovery because Joelle had not felt any contractions and had no spotting.

After reviewing the results with the perinatologist, I explained to Joelle and Bryan some of the potential concerns, including the possibility of incompetent cervix—when the cervix fails to remain closed and preterm birth can be threatened. Watchful care was necessary to prevent early labor. As they settled into a comfortably old plush couch in their living room, I drew a picture for them describing what that "watchful care" might mean: the importance of reducing physical exertion, eliminating lifting, avoiding sexual activity, and initiating a pattern of close observation by ultrasound to identify any changes in the cervix going forward.

To a woman who preferred a relaxed, sedentary life, this news would be inconvenient; but to Joelle—who, like her son, Evan, was a vibrant, social butterfly—this was a hard report. In addition to attending a Korean cooking class on Wednesday evenings, participating in a prenatal yoga and exercise class on Thrusday mornings, and occasionally a prenatal swim class at the "Y," she frequently planned trips to the zoo, a visit with friends, or play-dates with other moms and toddlers. Joelle and Bryan were also very active in their church, where he sang in the choir, and she helped facilitate a weekly Bible study. Being told all those activities might have to be shelved was a bit like having a large Plexiglas wall suddenly appear, with your life smiling back at you from the other side.

Not wanting to completely turn down her rhythm of life, Joelle agreed to significantly decrease her activity in hopes the negative report about her cervix would be turned around. So sans yoga, the pool, and the zoo, Joelle anxiously waited for the results of the next ultrasound, planned for three weeks later. Hoping for the best but unable to resist her strong first-born qualities to organize, she began to talk to her friends, her church, and her family, telling them that she, "Miss Independent," might need help soon. She shared with them the possibilities of needing their assistance with all the household chores, as well as taking care of her very active Evan.

Some few years ago, Joelle had been a finalist in Washington State's Beauty Pageant, and now she was scheduled to help judge the upcoming event in just two months' time. It was a lot of work and involved considerable effort and energy. We talked about how she might participate, even sitting in a chair onstage instead of walking to the podium. But in reality, this seemed a stretch...especially after the next ultrasound revealed an alarming and very discouraging change of her cervix, now 70 percent effected and one centimeter. Even though Joelle had greatly decreased her daily activity, her body had still taken many steps in the wrong direction.

When shown the results, it did not take long for Joelle and Bryan to understand the potential gravity of their situation. Now complete bed rest was prescribed, as the baby was only twenty-three weeks and simply could not yet be born. She asked many excellent question; Can I pick up Evan? Could I cook dinner? Can I vacuum? Can I take a walk? Can I make love to my husband? Should I stay in bed? Can I sit up to read and watch TV? And unfortunately, the answer to every one of these questions brought reality starkly home. In order to give her baby a good shot at life, Joelle was going to have to put hers completely and utterly on hold. She knew it would not be easy, but with the generous support and help of all those she garnered, she knew she could accomplish complete bed rest, except for her periodic visits to the perinatologist.

The next ultrasound revealed continued weakening, as the cervix was now 95 percent effaced and one and a half centimeters dilated, even in the face of drastically reduced activity. Knowing she was teetering on the edge of hospitalization, Joelle came to realize that "absolute bed rest" meant exactly that, although the bed could mean the couch. A horizontal posture was essential, nearly 100 percent of the time. Sitting up was no longer an option, as this caused contractions. Even trips to the bathroom brought on contractions. She learned to perform every daily task, even eating and drinking, completely on her back or side.

I made home visits to check on this sweet baby, growing so peacefully, unaware of the commitment to well-being that mom was making, *and* to check up on Joelle, to admire her persistence, her patience, her will to be prone so her baby could be born healthy. Joelle understood she had to get to "term," thirty-seven weeks, in order to deliver at home as she so strongly desired. She also was aware she needed to get as far as possible, in any case, in order to assure a healthy baby who would not need intensive or prolonged care for prematurity.

In my visits to her, I'd go in the kitchen and find a salad or a sandwich someone had made her or a pre-made dinner keeping warm in the oven. I'd watch Evan play around her, zooming cars along the braided edge of the couch, bringing his mom a book to read him, still enamored of *Frog and Toad*, learning that she could hug him but not pick him up. Evan must have understood something on his little two-year-old level, because he hovered near her happily, even protectively at times, and tolerated the stream of helpful friends, family—often strangers—who appeared at his front door daily. Only when daddy came home in the evening did he sometimes let the slats down, and express his little frustrations.

The perinatologist explained to Joelle and Bryan that he did not know whether her cervix would hold on and keep this baby in, or whether it would continue to complete dilation and effacement, with nothing left to hold together, thus allowing an open doorway for this baby. The nature of her condition was so unpredictable, and he was not able to forecast anything, not even a reasonable guess.

He did, however, imply it was highly unlikely, with the state of her cervix at the moment, that she would carry the baby to the desired thirty-seven weeks. At this point, Joelle's first and foremost priority was keeping the baby inside her belly as long as possible, and she wondered if she would have to give up her dream of a home birth.

But very soon, her hard work of doing no work began to pay off. At the next appointment with the perinatologist, the ultrasound finally gave some great news! After a few weeks of the absolute bed rest, her cervix actually "fattened up." Because the bed rest protected the cervix from any pressure, it had strengthened; it didn't bulge out when she coughed but appeared to act like a normal cervix and eventually backed off to 50 percent effaced and one centimeter dilated. The relief this couple felt was euphoric, as they knew their strategy was bringing in the kind of results they wanted, and they were reenergized to continue the journey.

Joelle and Bryan were willing to take the hard route, not allowing the gamble, and simply made things work. Bryan made breakfast, put boxed lunches for Evan and Joelle together, and ate gratefully whatever lovely surprise dinner he found in the refrigerator when he came home from work. TV dinners, mostly homemade, became standard fare for their nightly routine, and prayer a daily reminder that God had them firmly in his gasp. For these two passionately driven people, who loved to serve others it was a bit difficult to now be the receivers, but what a precious lesson to learn.

Finally, thirty-seven weeks arrived without further incident, and Joelle was permitted to get up, practically leaping off the couch. Such a long wait it had been! Joelle exclaimed, "Wouldn't it be grand if labor started right now?!" Well, that day came and went and the next day and the next, along with the lesson that there is a certain timing to this business that seems to have a mind of its own. At thirty-seven weeks and five days, the first sputterings of labor commenced, and soon Joelle was in active labor, thrilled but having the typical second thoughts about labor that seem to come along with the first "real" contractions.

It is a great blessing that labor dances along to a fiery rhythm all on its own. Joelle got in step with this miraculous and beautiful dance, leaning against Bryan as the contraction built up, making shushing sounds at the peak, exhaling with relief and a sigh signaling the end, grateful for that momentary respite between pains so welcome, yet so intense. Her contractions swelled and receded, building gradually to a predictable pattern every two and half minutes, lasting seventy seconds of crescendo and decrescendo, and releasing Joelle at the end to an almost free-fall sleep.

In labor, time seems to stand outside the room, beyond the tunnel vision of the laboring mom. Minutes can feel like hours, and hours can seem like mere moments. But right on course, the pattern of labor changes, kind of like putting on a thirty-three rpm record instead of a seventy-eight, and that unmistakable urge to push begins.

"What a great relief," Joelle exclaimed, as she took a deep, down-to-your-toes breath and felt the baby shift down her spine, down her pelvis, and down her birth canal. Bryan stood next to me, holding Joelle's hand and allowing her to press her leg against him for support. I could almost feel his heart beat with anticipation and excitement as he watched Joelle's face for the signal for the next contraction. He readied himself to be there for her in whatever way she needed. With the next contraction, Joelle heralded her push with a great Sound of a Trumpet, then captured that noise and silently put her whole effort into bringing this miracle as close to out as possible.

Bryan and I could see the baby's black hair, all wet and matted to the top of the head. With the next contraction, we could see the skin under that glorious head of hair wrinkle up as Joelle brought her baby closer. On the fifth push, this lovely little head emerged, with a face all scrunched up, starting to grimace, and with tiny fingers showing at the neck to tell us a hand will come with the shoulders. Seconds later, the shoulders and hand, then body, then legs, then toes, those Popsicle Toes, all plopped out into Daddy's waiting arms, prefaced by a delightful and lusty yell.

This gorgeous baby girl made such a splash, like an Olympic swimmer after the starting gun. Sometimes babies squirt themselves out, just plopping into waiting hands. Some babies work their way out, almost like they're layered in sticky tape, and each centimeter of body comes out with a little more effort. Some babies truly fly out, as if on wings of an angel. Don't blink or you'll miss it! Some babies twist and turn, even all the way around, as if they wanted that 360-degree view before leaving their old home for a new one. And some babies come out gurgling and sputtering, like waterfalls over rocks below. This little girl arrived in a rush, landing with her sweet, perfect body and soul entirely intact to be welcomed with tears of relief and joy. All the work, all the patience, all the pain, and all the waiting; worth every moment for this new life that will change the world.

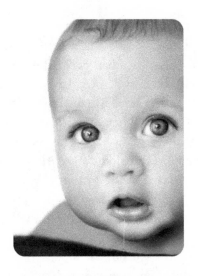

Giving All for One

Adversity can transform a life
Heartache clears the decks, cleans the plate
Life's unnecessary trappings fall away
Elemental emotions stand out in bold relief.
The timbre of one's soul
The mournful echoes of sorrow
Reverberate 'cross the taut strings of love.
In the vagaries of life
The twists and turns of circumstance
Sometimes we choose
Sometimes we are chosen
Sometimes the choice is made for us.

My friends Anna and Jacob came to see me at the beginning of their pregnancy, an unplanned event and a great surprise to them both. Now in their late thirties, they had decided not to have children and were fully engaged in the lives of an artist and musician. Anna was an accomplished pianist, and Jacob pursued his painting with studios in several different countries. They enjoyed their bohemian existence, and upon meeting them, it was clear this recent positive pregnancy test had turned their lives upside down. All their plans for the next decades now required major alterations. One thing, however, was certain; Anna and Jacob possessed a deep love and regard for each other. I knew they would grow to embrace this very surprising turn of events.

On our first visit, we talked at length about pregnancy, its challenges, its triumphs, what to expect, how to prepare, what to eat, what not to eat, and so forth. Like children learning a new language, Anna and Jacob tested the waters of different ideas, thoughts, concepts, and philosophies. They wanted the best of all possible worlds for this baby; a great portent for the future, I thought.

Four weeks later, when Anna and Jacob arrived for their second appointment, I was pleased to see an entirely renewed expression. Anna was radiant with her newfound vision of motherhood and shared with me how she and Jacob had been transformed in the last few weeks as the reality of becoming parents settled into their hearts. She told me how desires neither of them even knew they possessed had surfaced from within, and the thoughts they once had about parenthood being a chore and a burden had turned into feelings of excitement, challenge, and most of all, joy. I was thrilled at this complete conversion and expressed to her that her feelings had only just begun; just wait until you see your precious little baby face-to-face!

How delighted they were to hear their baby's heartbeat at eleven weeks. This is always a distinct mark in the pregnancy for the mother and father as the miraculous idea of a baby is transformed into a tangible metronomic sound. This is especially true for first-time parents, and Anna and Jacob were no exception. Then, at our fifteenth week visit, they informed me they needed to travel on a business trip and expected to be away for several months. It was arranged that they would receive care there, including the requisite twenty-week ultrasound to identify their baby's growth and wellbeing. They also wanted to know if this little "bean" was boy or a girl. They looked forward to this ultrasound and promised they would report to me as soon as they knew all the results.

During the diagnostic ultrasound, it was determined their first child was to be a son! Both Anna and Jacob's eyes filled with tears as they watched the miracle of this life moving around inside his little home. As the radiology technician continued, the baby's fingers and toes were identified and counted, his heart was examined, and his spine was carefully reviewed. All these structures appeared normal.

Then the technician became quiet and focused as she moved the wand around the outside of Anna's pregnancy belly. She appeared to be looking for something. She excused herself for a moment, and the silence that remained in the examining room upon her exit was deafening. Anna and Jacob knew something was amiss, and they could not utter a word for fear of expressing something unimaginable.

The technician returned with the radiologist, also a perinatologist, who took the wand and moved it slowly over Anna's abdomen. Anna closed her eyes and lost herself in the loud sound of her anxiously beating heart. Jacob's hand tightened around hers as they waited for a verdict that seemed to become graver which each passing moment. Finally, the doctor broke the silence with soft, painful words, "I'm so sorry." He then explained to them his findings, measuring his words with care so that the parents would hear and understand. A heavy blanket of sorrow filled the room.

Perfect in every other way, Anna and Jacob's little boy had no kidneys. Called Potter's Syndrome, this uncommon malady is a lethal condition. While a baby remains alive within his mother, it is difficult for him to grow well and impossible for him to live outside the uterus.

There is no remedy. Anna and Jacob were devastated.

They planned, in the great grief of the moment, to terminate this pregnancy. Carrying such a baby to term and enduring the labor and delivery seemed impossibly hard to both of them. However,

Anna's placenta appeared to be covering the cervix, and termination was not an option at that time. Perhaps the placenta would move away from the cervix as her uterus grew later in the pregnancy, but Anna would have to wait weeks, maybe months, to determine the viability of this option. Anna and Jacob returned to their Northwest home to wait and to mourn.

And then a miraculous thing happened. This required delay, this sentence of doom for the next two or three months, turned into a great blessing in the midst of painful tragedy. Instead of growing emotionally removed from this child with no hope for survival, Anna and Jacob began to fall in love with their baby. They named him Orion, and they loved him more with each passing day.

Reading that babies inside are able to hear, Anna began to play her music for Orion, daily composing songs for him, singing to him, and feeling him kick inside. Jacob's tenderness for Anna, and now for his unborn son, moved his friends to tears. He would read aloud, tapping the cadence of his words on the confines of Anna's abdomen. The couple purposed to find areas of humor so they could laugh aloud in order for Orion to hear, and they spoke of their unconditional love to him every night before going to sleep. Jacob and Anna decided to rejoice in the little time they had and began to plan for his birth with the greatest of care.

Both had begun to find the inner peace and strength to cope with this situation and at one of our appointments, Anna described how they had journeyed to their current frame of mind as well as how they had been managing the emotions of disappointment. They held each other often, cried when they needed to, took long walks together, and slowly came to accept this news. Then, they began to talk and to plan about how they would spend the remaining time with Orion. They chose to treasure every day of life they had together, determined that his birth would be welcomed with a celebration, in the midst of natural sadness.

So Anna continued to maintain her health, eating especially well, choosing home-grown foods in season, finding organic items where available, drinking good water, taking leisurely walks along the gravelly shores of Puget Sound near her home, feeling the gentle waves lap rhythmically against her feet. She shared with me that it was moments like these, of reflective contemplation as she watched the sun quickly disappear behind the peaks of the Olympic Mountains, that gave her respite and renewed strength to her soul.

Anna and Jacob discussed endlessly what they thought Orion might look like. Would he have her ears, with a gentle dip on their edge? Would he have hair, golden with delicious strawberry highlights like Anna, or the chocolate brown of Jacob, minus the sprinkles of gray? Surely he would be tall, since both his parents viewed the world from almost six feet. Mostly they longed to feel his sweet breath on their cheeks, to kiss his skin, examine his long fingers and toes. Each day seemed to slip forever into evening, and then morning came, with new waiting.

Jacob intensified his painting, finding new inspiration as creative thoughts flowed through his talented hands onto his canvases. He again had to be out of town on business for several weeks, and Anna filled some of her time making caps, knitted with fine soft yarn in multi-shades of blue and green and mauve. Most of her recreation, however, was spent sitting at her piano composing songs and singing lilting melodies each day for little Orion. It seemed to them both as if all of life's love and attention must be compressed into this small moment of time, so little of it left, and yet so much to say, to sing, to compose, to express.

At each prenatal visit, we would visit and sometimes cry, tears welling up suddenly at a comment, a thought turned around, a wish unrevealed. I had several conversations with my obstetrician, who monitored placental location for Anna and helped her understand what was happening inside her uterus. Anna and Jacob knew that because Orion had no kidneys, he couldn't process amniotic fluid, so his little "house" was cramped, preventing him from growing much, from having the proper lung expansion, and from turning head down when we would usually expect that at about thirty weeks. Anna learned she should expect an early labor, perhaps by thirty-four weeks, and as time drew near, she began to prepare.

They desired to deliver Orion in the quiet, serene environment of their small home in town. We reviewed their plans with the obstetrician, and the necessary medical and legal arrangements were made. Jacob had newly remodeled their bungalow, and now Anna added little touches of grace wherever she could with marigolds and petunias on the windowsills, fresh grapes on the table, and silver picture frames awaiting their intended occupant.

Anna finally started labor, later than expected at nearly thirty-eight weeks. They had prepared a small repast for their friends. There were platters of carrots, broccoli, peas, cauliflower, and tiny tomatoes, pitchers of ice-cold lemonade and iced tea, and cashews and pecans to munch on. As her house filled with close friends and family, there was a palpable sense of anticipation. Anna and Jacob wanted to share this time with those they loved, who loved them back; and the house seemed full to bursting.

We had hoped for a quick birth, a smaller baby, an earlier delivery. Orion was still breech, of course, and to start labor, he pushed his little foot out as if to tell us the race had begun. Anna, Jacob, and I talked in the privacy of their bedroom, and I asked them to consider a change of plans. A compound single footling breech presentation, one leg up and one leg down, was troubling. This baby might only take a single breath, and I thought the best opportunity for them to meet him, even if only momentarily, was to consider a cesarean section. While his heart tones were strong and steady now, it seemed doubtful to me that Orion would live through the natural rigors of this breech birth.

Anna paused as if holding her breath. She clearly understood that she could choose to deliver her baby at her home, but in doing so, she might be giving up the chance to share with Orion the precious seconds of life he might be given. On the other hand, a cesarean section was a major surgery for her, and it would not improve the baby's outcome. However, after all these months of waiting, her desire to share life with Orion prompted an immediate, clear, definitive, and emphatic. "Yes!" Her husband agreed. We talked with the obstetrician, and he assured them he would be waiting for them when they arrived.

Jacob quickly began to gather up some extra clothes for Anna, their camera, and a few selected important items for Orion: a knitted cap, a blanket crocheted by his grandmother and a soft stuffed lamb the color of buttercups. Jacob and Anna briefly explained to their gathered guests about the change in plans, and promptly we all were off to the hospital. The nurses and assistants were waiting, the obstetrician expressed his kind and thoughtful sentiments to Anna and Jacob, and soon Anna was prepared for the cesarean section. It seemed as if the entire group of assembled helpers had a single focus of making Anna's experience safe and tender, and giving Orion the opportunity for that one breath.

Anna requested minimal medication for nausea; she wanted to be as alert as she could in the next few moments. The surgeon carefully made his incision, talking to Anna and Jacob so they would be ready to greet Orion the instant he was born. At long last, he emerged; beautifully, perfect, and small. This was a moment frozen in time when the surgeon handed Orion to the nurse, who gave him to Anna, and in that passage, he made one small cry. And then he was gone.

Anna and Jacob held their son for a long, long time as her incision was repaired, and preparations made to take her to recovery. Many pictures were taken, permanent memories of an impermanent time. The hospital supported Anna and Jacob in many wonderful ways, assuring her as long as she needed to have Orion with her. She took footprints, handprints, pictures, a lock of his dark hair, more pictures, kisses unending, cradling him in her arms, singing to him strains of melodies sung months ago. Two days later, Anna and Jacob were able to say good-bye.

The next week, the memorial service held at Anna and Jacob's home was filled with those same friends and family who had gathered to greet Orion. Now they assembled to express their sadness and tremendous respect for the gratitude with which Anna and Jacob had imbued this entire experience. Their home, suffused with soft light, was a haven for everyone as both Mom and Dad spoke of the great gift they called Orion. Though here for only a moment, he had a powerful impact upon everyone around him, as his life reminded us all what really matters.

At a crossroads, this couple had met adversity, and it became a catalyst for good. These parents had moved forward, tentatively at first and finally with confidence and purpose, as their unconditional love forged a path for Orion's brief existence. They also provided a roadmap for their own private struggles. What came of their sorrow was considerable good.

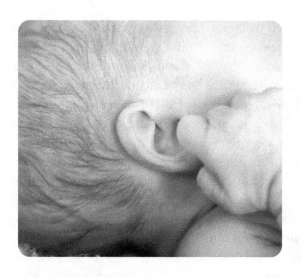

Midnight Adventures

When the bustle of the day has subsided and little ones are asleep, the cat's been put outside, and the dog's been sent to his bed; that's the time for babies to knock on the door. Soon my phone rings. I must admit I have always found these nighttime calls pleasant, as I love the quiet and serenity of that moment and am instantly awake with anticipation and expectation for the voice on the other end. A call at that hour could only mean a baby.

On a snowy night in January 1979, the phone jangled in my ear at about 1:15 a.m. This time it was Nadine, sweet young Nadine, whose voice trembled with each contraction as she paused between phrases, describing her labor. She was barely out of her teens but not out of her opinions, and she had a beautiful crafted, though lengthy, list of exactly how she wanted this birth to proceed. Of course, this baby was surely its mother's child wanted this birth to proceed. Of course, this baby was surely its mother's child, with a mind of its own, determined to make an appearance in the midst of a wild storm that had blanketed the whole area with several feet of fresh snow. We all had been surprise earlier in the evening by the big swirling flakes—as big as nickels—that fell in unremitting sheets for the next many hours, because the Puget Sound area rarely experiences anything like a blizzard. Because it is nestled between two mountain ranges, our climate is fairly mild year—round, never too hot and never too cold, though with more than enough rain.

By midnight, the ground was white with enormous mounds of whipped cream, softening all the corners and edges of the fields that fell away to the south of us, and then suddenly butted up against enormous trees wearing their robes of white, with long sleeves of white flowing down to the ground.

Nadine had awakened just shortly before 1:00 to the unmistakable rush of fluid, clear and sweet smelling, like a newborn, and she knew her time had come. The contractions had come on strong almost immediately, and she could barely tell me about it. I told her I would be there as soon as possible and continued to talk to her with reassurance while I gathered my clothes, equipment, oxygen tank, keys, charts, notes, and map. Within minutes, it seemed, I was at the door ready to charge out into the night.

There, standing in front of me, fully dressed, alert, and serious, was my husband. Without a word, he picked up my things, put them into our car, got into the driver's seat, and started the engine. I couldn't describe my feelings, so full of gratitude that this man understood instantly the danger a trip out into the darkness of this night might represent. No sleep for him, no rest except to take me himself, assuring me of his guidance, his support, his concern, and his love. To add to this midnight drama, I was seven months pregnant myself, with a full belly, anticipating another ten-pound baby like the three before. While we drove slowly over the quieted roads, I could feel the stirrings of activity and put my hands on my belly to catch the movement. Nothing can replace that feeling. It's as fine as the snow drifting in the wind.

When we could catch our breath, we laughed at the sight of the two of us, braving unreasonable weather, bundled up against the elements so only our dark eyes flashed, snow so deep that the interstate freeway was nearly impassable, hoping we didn't get stuck in the drifts that were blowing across the roads, the car heater doing yeoman's service to keep us warm and blasting so noisily we had to shout over it, but oh, what joy at the end of this bumpy ride.

When we got to Nadine's home, she was in the throws of active labor. My husband brought my things to the door for me and then retreated to the car, leaving the woman to the privacy of her warm home. So unobtrusive, so decorous, careful about everyone's personal space; he had thoughtfully brought a bundle of warm blankets to wrap up in, along with a down pillow, and there he camped for the duration. No inducement could get him to change his mind, so we left him to the snug confines of the automobile.

No one knows how long the dance lasts, when this baby will decide to give up its old home and embrace the welcoming new one. But with the rising morning light, his beautiful squall could be heard through the windows onto the silent snow outside. What a glorious noise, this raucous wakening. I looked outside and could see my husband stirring slightly, knowing from our many conversations how glad he would be for safe and happy arrival of another newborn.

Several hours later, with breakfast made, I emerged from this warm and cozy home to my waiting husband, with muffins in hand, for the peaceful and secure ride home. He would leave for work, if the roads were kind, while I plunged into paperwork to keep ahead of the beast. Paperwork, like snow, can bury you, and there's no solution to it but to tackle it head on. But as I typed the baby's name—James Edward—onto the birth certificate with my little Royal typewriter, I thanked God for such a man to keep me safe and give me the space to do this amazingly delightful work…followed quickly by the blessed rest of a well-earned nap.

The life of a midwife can definitely seem like a string of days all squished into one, adhered together by a series of naps. There is never a shortage of stories of these midnight adventures. Here's another one!

The still of the night was once again abruptly disturbed. Earlier, the culprit was a strong end-of-summer storm that knocked out the power to much of the South Puget Sound area, and this time it was a firm and loud pounding on our front door. Because of the storm, we were just now, at midnight settling into the beds of our little country house on the edge of Church Lake, only to pop back up from the sound of a visitor. The gentleman at the door was the local policeman, reporting that a patient of mine who was beginning labor was unable to get through on the telephone. This was September of 1977, and as the world had not yet been introduced to mainstream cell phones and pagers, landlines were the primary source of communication.

I graciously thanked the officer for coming to get me at this very early hour, and I quickly dressed and loaded myself along with all my supplies into our little 1964 Ford Falcon. Traveling down the Old Sumner Buckley Highway at that time was vastly different than today; this area was primarily pasture land with cows grazing quietly in one area, horses in their nighttime repose in another, and owls hooting occasionally in the treetops at the corners of the fields. The moon emerged bright and bold over the landscape, with lingering hints of the previous storm.

I could see the beautiful beginnings of fall, leaves already turning brown and the smell of hay lingering heavily on the ground. By now it was two in the morning, and only the stars kept me company as I wandered in my thoughts about this upcoming birth. I was excited for this much-desired baby and wondered how Emily and Josh would do together. The pregnancy had been easy and uncomplicated, and she had just about met her due date head on.

Several miles later, the road curved softly to the right, and the full moon came into view, magically lighting the road and pasture with a brilliant whitish glow. And there in the bright moonlight in the middle of the road stood Corliss's prized bull, all 2,000 pounds of him. For a brief second, I gasped at his magnificence, and then the next, wondered when he was going to move himself out of the way of my car. It seemed as if everything passed into slow motion as my car plummeted toward this enormous beast, who just stared at me as if to say, "Lady, I own this road…go around me."

The only problem was, there was no going around him, no negotiating the territory, no dirt shoulder on the side of the road, and no way to slip-slide away past this bull, monstrous in size and stubbornness. He continued to look at me, utterly unfazed, as my car hurled directly into the massive animal. The impact threw me over the fence and into the midst of a startled herd of Holsteins.

The Falcon was a total wreck, the engine resting nicely in the front seat and the hood standing straight up as if to hide the shattered windshield. After a few very deep breaths, I realized gratefully I had not been injured and collected my wits, which were flung far and wide. The realization of a patient in labor settled once again in my mind, and I wriggled myself and my birthing bag out of the wreckage, climbed over the fence, and began to walk the mile to the police station in this little town of Bonney Lake. I had no other options, as in this age before cell phones, my biggest dilemma was finding anyone for assistance. The likelihood of seeing another car was small, and even if I did, would it be safe for me to flag it down? Also, there was no use trying to wake any neighbors, because there were very few scattered here and there in the countryside. I assumed the police station would be my best bet; however, when I arrived at the small structure that housed the police and firemen, a sign stated the office was closed for lack of funds. I was at a loss.

Just then a car came around the corner, its lights bright in the blackness of night. At first sight of me walking alongside this deserted road with a suitcase and my black hair long enough to sit on, I wondered if the driver would think I was a runaway. But when he came closer, I was surprised to see it was not only a police vehicle but also the very same Angel in the Night who had come to my door earlier! Upon meeting, it was with great relief for us both, and he was kind enough to take me to the birth twenty-five miles away in Spanaway.

Emily and Josh were waiting for me, surprised to see an official vehicle parked in their driveway. After making arrangements for transportation home later, I sent Mr. Officer away with many thanks and promised to report on the results of the night. Emily labored well. Her coping method was to sing at the top of her lungs when the contractions got intense, and then to drift off nearly to sleep in between. Her song was definitely all her own, full of trills and vibrato. Josh and I watched and listened quietly to her, respecting her space and her needs. Along about time for breakfast, Emily was ready to get this baby boy out. She hollered, she shouted, she sang, she yelled, she delivered a nine-pound baby they named Wolf, a fitting moniker for a strapping young man ready for breakfast.

Back at the ranch, Corliss had his big bull rendered before the first light of day crested the hill beyond the barn. My old Ford Falcon was also rendered un-repairable. I was sad to see her go; we had been down many roads and arrived at many births together. As I have traveled that section of the old two-lane highway over the next thirty-odd years, watching housing developments replace the dilapidated red barn and businesses grow up alongside, I frequently recalled that lonely drive in the fall of 1977. I am ever grateful for the happy outcome for all.

The Perfect Baby

"I don't care if it's a boy or a girl, just so long as it's healthy." A common sentiment, expressed openly by both fathers and mothers-to-be, describes the normal emotions of expectation and attachment to this stranger, their baby. Often one parent or the other really does have a temporary preference, but as soon as they learn by ultrasound whether baby is a boy or a girl, they are most of the time completely satisfied and overjoyed—and thrilled to know all the structures appear normal. Surely they'll get a piano for Little Button, because the world won't be the same after this baby's Grand Entrance.

So I was especially moved one fine summer afternoon when a mother about fifteen weeks into her sixth pregnancy said to me, without reservation, "I want whatever baby I am blessed to have." This was such a different remark from the usual expression, that it startled me at first. Of course, it's true, and truth stands on its own. I knew Marcia well and respected her devotion to her family and her quiet unassuming manner. She was tough as nails on any issue of character, but she had a tenderness that often evoked tears.

We discussed at length what Marcia meant by her remark, and she reiterated that she would be happy with "whatever baby I am blessed to have." We talked about problems that occasionally arise, cardiac issues, structural defects, limb deformities. Marcia knew that I had had a few patients whose babies had a lethal condition and could not live. She had a conviction, which I had come over time to appreciate, that all life is precious. Sometimes we get nearly unlimited access to these children made in God's image. Sometimes they grace our lives for the briefest period, but their memory lingers forever.

We talked about how the prescription for a good pregnancy goes like this; "Love each other, and do good." We agreed that if this is the driving force in one's life, every decision will be a positive one, and the result will be the best it can be!

Marcia and I had worked together through five previous pregnancies, and she and her husband, Dalton, were thrilled with each new addition. They thought this pregnancy might be their last, and they savored each moment.

Their youngest child, Jon, now nearly three years old, was born on Thanksgiving Day after a wandering labor that took its sweet time. It began to snow lightly in the night, wispy flakes blowing around in the small gusts, swirling with capricious intention and dusting the trees and evergreen bushes with the merest coating of white. Hers could be called a "putzy" labor, rather like the snowfall, except Marcia was quite content with contractions sporadically spaced throughout the night and into the morning. Dalton seemed fine with the pace as well and diligently warmed her cup with chamomille tea from time to time.

The embers of the Franklin fireplace in the den had softened to an orange glow, and the faintest light brightened the morning sky through the snowy haze, when Marcia declared, "Now it's time." Without further ado, Jon made his entrance after two sturdy pushes, and soon there was resounding thunderous applause. His father and the other boys had no lack of enthusiasm, even at 6:00 a.m. on that wintry day. It seemed even the rafters vibrated with the shouts of boy noise, a chorus of delight led by the dad. Only Ben, then the youngest, stayed asleep on the cot in the next room through the peaceful commotion of birth.

What soon became apparent in the hours following his birth was that Jon most likely had Downs Syndrome. Marcia and Dalton were surprised, as they had decided against an ultrasound in this pregnancy and so had no earlier notice. But this remarkable couple was not dismayed, as they truly felt "blessed to have any baby given to them." As Jon nursed, though with a bit less vigor than his older siblings had done, we arranged for baby Jon to have a pediatric examination at 9:00 a.m. He was kept warm, snuggled cozily with his mother, and we all watched him carefully for the next hour or so. He soon fell asleep on her chest as she hummed her favorite hymn, "How Great Thou Art."

Jon David grew to be chubby and cute, with fat cheeks and a tuft of fair hair that made him look like an advertisement for holiday cookies. He did have Downs, but his siblings thought he was just fine, the boys delighted with another brother; and Susan, the elder sister, was pleased to retain the role of Prime (and only) Princess.

Over the next three years, Jon advanced, slowly in height but by leaps and bounds in personality. He had an impish nature that both delighted and sometimes frustrated his brothers and was tenderly amusing to his parents. He was the darling of his family, and everyone just doted on him.

It is hard to describe the effect this little boy with Downs had on his family. His open nature and innocent heart created a cement that bonded his family, even the extended ones. His uncles Joe and Barney, aunt Vicki, and older cousins Melinda and Cody had been somewhat reserved, even awkward in the presence of this baby with Downs. But soon they also fell head-over-heels, over-the-top, pie-in-the-sky in love with this boy with the shock of snow-white hair and brilliant blue eyes. His smile filled his face and flooded their hearts. Each member jostled for the privilege of playing with him, lying on the rug with him, singing to him, changing him, learning to feed him, and talking to him. Jon looked out of eyes of innocence, watching each person with complete trust and confidence. He was plain swamped with affection and attention. And so he grew some every day.

Now after several years, Marcia and Dalton were preparing for another new little one. Jon's birth and life had given each member of the family the profoundest confidence that "we'll take whatever we're blessed with." Susan was almost twelve years old by this time, a sweet girl with the emerging motherly instincts so tender at her age. She had relished being "second mom" to Little Jon, and now she was looking forward to this new baby with great anticipation, confident it would be a sister for her. She thought Merrillee was the prettiest name and spoke it often in little whispers of hope.

Their new baby was born on a wind-blown weekend in March, definitely "in like a lion." Susie was speechless at the sight of her new baby sister; then she shrieked like a girl and called the baby in her mother's arms Merrillee. Jon waddled over and patted her. "Gently, gently," said his mother. Each older boy took his turn with a kiss or a pat. Then dad raised her up to his shoulder, thanked God, and gave his traditional war-whoop of joy.

In the weeks that followed, as I observed Marcia and Dalton with their family, I was reminded of another treasured experience. SheriAnn was a spunky seventeen-year-old and a daughter of a good friend who had birthed several children with me. Now it was SheriAnn's turn, and she was certainly up for "baling hay," which we had affectionately come to call the work of birth. Her dark eyes sparkled with delight when she spoke of this baby, though there were tears that gathered at the edges of her delicious "m&m" brown eyes when she nodded yes, she would be raising this baby alone. Only the slight flush of her cheeks revealed her silent sorrow. Still, SheriAnn would not consider what her life might be without this baby, though she honestly acknowledged that completing her senior year following the birth would be though. In addition, she was dealing with her challenges and sadness at having to give up her college dreams and the scholarship she had won in theatre.

The girlie baby she would name Emily, and she expected her within the month, just after the close of the school year, ending her junior year. She recalled her last summer, so full of excitement and hope, evening walks along the pier, dates with friends, movies almost unending, jazz concerts in the park, her whole future dancing on the stage in front of her, sending sparklers of fireworks overhead whenever she thought about her dream. Growing up, Sheri had loved dance above all things and had spent many hours in high school with a drama/dance troupe. She had thoughts of traveling with her energetic group of eight best-friends, young men and women she had known almost since kindergarten. They had all often talked about raising funds with their performances and helping orphaned children. But now her life had taken a different turn, and all her energies were engaged in caring for this baby, soon to be delivered.

The law of unintended consequences isn't always a hammer blow, however. Sometimes important lessons are learned, and maturity and sweetness are the result. SheriAnn started labor the Monday after class graduation. At first, she felt the mild cramping of her uterus, sort of like the muscle tightening she recognized with her flips and leg kicks in a rigorous dance routine. Sheri thought it felt like a fist balled up inside and began to track the pattern after several hours. When she noticed her gaze drifting to the clock every four or five minutes, she called to say things had started. With her usual good humor and a small trembling in her voice, she said, "Let the games begin!"

SheriAnn's labor was fairly straightforward. Her uterine contractions gradually increased, and as they got closer and longer, they also got stronger. SheriAnn began to pace and set the pattern of her labor dance. Her diameter of light spanned about twenty feet and encircled two chairs, one low stool, a loveseat, two lamps, and an end table. The coffee table had long since been relegated to the back room to leave more space for this important path. She inhaled at the first lamp, began a slow whistle as she passed the chair and ottoman, blew lightly as she moved beyond the loveseat and end table, and opened her eyes in relief as she rounded the chair and tall lamp by the door. SheriAnn's mom and I watched in silent awe as Sheri gathered her skirts of courage with each contraction. She would put her head down, face into the wind of pain, looking behind closed lids at the blissful rest beyond, and then open her big brown eyes and exhale with a deep sigh at the end.

Beads of sweat began to form on her upper lip. She had tied her hair up in a ribbon of blue, but little wisps of hair escaped and stuck to her neck. Her light summer shift was damp and clung to her skin as she moved with each contraction. From time to time, she quickly drank a deep mouthful of water as she passed the loveseat on her circular path. Only a slight moan escaped her lips when the contraction seemed to last beyond the measured bars of this music. A diaphanous smile wafted across her face and turned up the corners of her mouth as she felt the baby kick a little. It was the best dance of her life, and pretty soon it would be done.

Eventually, a great heaviness began to sit between her knees. SheriAnn felt the tilt of her baby as she prepared herself for her baby's grand entrance. The urge to push began as a catch in her throat, but soon Sheri was captured by the deep guttural groan that signaled the final movement of this symphony. Snare drums and tambourines and violins and French horns and a grand piano all together couldn't equal the intensity and import of that final push when Emily emerged, all wet and glistening. SheriAnn later told me how transformed she felt at that exact moment, when Emily gave her first cry.

That Emily had Downs Syndrome surprised SheriAnn and her family. This teenager didn't fit the usual stereotype of the "elderly gravida." It's not well known that Downs and other differences occur throughout the age range of pregnant women. Sheri's family had a good cry, mostly at the loss of normal societal expectations for Emily and for the worry that her extended medical needs would bring.

SheriAnn, on the other hand, was simply overwhelmed with this new being; and every time Sheri picked up Emily, held her close, smelled her breath, felt the soft downy hair on her skin, and listened to her breathing as she slept next to her, she loved her more. Her motherly instincts grabbed hold of her heart with fierceness. Many moms look back and wonder where that ferocity comes from, and they marvel at the love that bubbles up out of the deepest core of their being for their child. I think there is an added measure of attachment that occurs with these fragile and dependent children.

Their differences from other children mean a lifetime of work, care, hope, faith, trial, responsibility, love, and joy. Still, they give back as good as they get!

Emily required several surgeries, and with each event, the purse strings of Sheri's spirit tightened. As Emily's heart was repaired in stages, SheriAnn's heart was healed and strengthened as well. She was a remarkably devoted mother, though still as teenager, and she approached motherhood with a singleness of mind and purpose that was amazing. She was filled with gratitude for her own mother, grandma to Emily, for the constancy and attention she focused on her grandchild; but she never shirked her own responsibilities, and she made sure she was actively present for every decision, every event, every turn required to raise this child.

By the time Emily was three years old, she had come through some tough times, medical events, surgeries, and many night vigils that her mom and grandparents held as they watched her with great care. She possessed such tenacity, and her indomitable spirit was infectious. People made room for this little girl with blond curls, two deep dimples like canyons, lovely almond shaped eyes of green, and a heart that she wore "on her sleeve."

And her mom also grew every day. With the ever present help of her parents, SheriAnn managed in the bustle of caring for this precious child to make room for her studies. While it took her two years, she finished high school and then enrolled in the local community college, with an eye on a nursing career. She had completed her prerequisite and decided to celebrate with an evening watching the local baseball farm team for the Seattle Mariners at Cheney Stadium. Emily loved the rare hotdog splurge and was content to sit on her mom's lap while SheriAnn and her parents enjoyed the noise of the crowd, the small-town feel of the game, and the lovely summer air at this outdoor venue.

Sitting down the row was a young man with a boy about five years old, munching popcorn and shucking peanut shells. This father and son duo laughed easily and seemed quite comfortable together. SheriAnn struck up a conversation as she passed another bag of popcorn from the vendor down the aisle to him. Randy and his son were also out for an evening's fun, and now his interest was piqued by this lovely girl and her family. They talked over the roar of the crowd and came to find much in common. Randy was the sole parent-in-tow for his son, Wyatt. Sheri watched him out of the corner of her eye and delighted that Wyatt's peanut antics both intrigued and amused her daughter, Emily.

In due time, Randy and Sheri began a year-long courtship and were married with her parents' blessings late the following summer. They had two children together with me, plus two makes four—a full house. From time to time, I've overheard Sheri comment quietly in soft conversations with her friends that though she brought Emily to birth, it was her profound belief that Emily had saved her life. And isn't that the truth for all of us? These babies—our children, grandchildren, nieces, nephews, and friends—miraculous, innocent, and sweet, are most often our link to God. They define us, they keep us pliable, they enrich us, and they strengthen us.

For me, over all these years, every birth is my favorite. The baby that just fell into my arms is the best. The glory of God shines in every sweet face of these lovely children made in His image. They are, without a doubt, *Heaven in My Hands*.

About the Author

Practicing for four decades and catching more than 4,000 babies, Nancy Spencer is one of the longest practicing midwives in the nation today. Her passion for midwifery—for moms, their babies, and the care of families in a childbirth setting—began to take shape in the mid-1960s. She came into contact with a number of alternative health care providers. And these relationships helped form the basis for a new approach to health, especially to childbirth.

In 1967, shortly after her first son's birth, Nancy met Dr. Robert A. Bradley. He had recently written the widely influential book *Husband-Coached Childbirth*, which later became the foundation of The Bradley Method, a popular approach to natural childbirth. This relationship furthered Nancy's interest in the emerging movement of childbirth education and methods of natural childbirth that were beginning to awaken all over the nation.

Nancy completed her education at the University of Washington, earning her Bachelor of Arts, cum laude, with a degree in English Literature and an induction into Phi Beta Kappa. In 1970 Nancy was hired by Green River Community College and Olympic Community College in Washington State to create a curriculum of classes designed to educate the growing number of people who desired to know about alternative styles of labor and delivery, and to learn how they could be more actively involved in the process of unmedicated labor and birth. Nancy taught these classes throughout the community for fifteen years.

During the 1970's Nancy apprenticed with a physician who owned a stand-alone birth clinic in Washington. Situated in the center of bustling city and surrounded by towering evergreens, this clinic was a haven in a serene setting, and Nancy assisted many births there.

At the same time, Nancy's grandfather-in-law, then serving as a Washington State Legislator and Chairman of the Social and Health Services Committee in the House of Representatives, sponsored midwifery legislation at Nancy's request. Dr. A. A. Adams was ably assisted by a group of women, midwives, consumers, and other professionals in the writing of what eventually became the current Washington State midwifery law. This law has served as a model for legislation for other states throughout the nation.

In 1981 Nancy enrolled in the second class at Seattle Midwifery School, completing this program for direct entry midwives 1983. This school, now part of Bastyr University, continues to enjoy an international reputation, and to be in the forefront of excellent midwifery education, offering myriad programs in support of women and families.

Nancy has served for many years as a Governor appointed representative in organizations such as the Washington State Midwifery Advisory Committee, and, since its inception, on the Washington State committee that provides and oversees professional liability for midwives and birth centers. In 2001 Nancy and another nurse midwife formed Professional Midwives Affiliation, a Washington State approved organization whose mission is to improve outcomes for mothers and babies under the care of midwives. This group includes midwives, obstetricians and perinatologists, childbirth educators, nurses, pediatricians, diabetic educators, and others, combining an interdisciplinary approach, continuing education, and protected peer review. Its goal is to provide optimum support for midwives who are interested in maintaining the highest standards and contributing to the wellbeing of midwifery clients—those precious moms and babies so loved by the midwives.

Nancy has a flourishing midwifery practice and, since 1994, in addition to her homebirth practice, she cares for moms babies at Lakeside Birth Center on beautiful Lake Tapps in Pierce County, Washington. Licensed by the State of Washington as a freestanding birth center, this lovely clinic serves the childbearing needs of families throughout the region.

CPSIA information can be obtained
at www.ICGtesting.com
Printed in the USA
BVHW030901140623
665885BV00002B/395

9 781953 699763